CURRENT PROBLEMS

General Editor:
Sir Ernest Barker, Litt.D.

GERMANY, RUSSIA
AND THE FUTURE

23

CURRENT PROBLEMS

General Editor: SIR ERNEST BARKER

GERMANY, RUSSIA AND THE FUTURE

A Psychological Essay

BY

J. T. MacCURDY, M.D., Sc.D.

*Fellow of Corpus Christi College, Lecturer
in Psychopathology, University of Cambridge*

CAMBRIDGE

AT THE UNIVERSITY PRESS

1944

CAMBRIDGE
UNIVERSITY PRESS

LONDON: BENTLEY HOUSE

NEW YORK, TORONTO, BOMBAY
CALCUTTA, MADRAS: MACMILLAN

All rights reserved

CONTENTS

PREFACE

The argument of this essay was sketched out and most of it was written before the Allied landing in Normandy. It seems advisable to state this because the reader may expect to find some comments on current events and therefore be disappointed with a discussion that considers the past and speculates about the future without, apparently, taking the present into the reckoning. But, when events are moving at great speed and publication is inevitably slow, only the daily press can deal with the present; and it is often out of date. Consequently I have had, reluctantly, to eliminate reference to what was happening at the moment, even though it might seem highly relevant, because by the time this work appeared the current event which seemed momentous might be dwarfed by still more catastrophic changes.

The object of my writing is to provoke thought concerning problems intertwined with decisions that will determine the course of civilization during the next few generations. There is no lack of publicly expressed opinions about policies to be pursued, but these emanate chiefly from opposing doctrinaire groups whose arguments proceed from theories as to what is socially or politically desirable rather than from the fruits of dispassionate search for the factors which have produced the problems to be solved. The collection and evaluation of the data in this field belong more to social psychology than to any other science, but that is not to say that psychology is yet in a position to publish recommendations based on well proven theory. Indeed as a science psychology cannot speak as yet because it is still in the stage of gathering data and making tentative hypotheses and has not yet advanced to the stage of established theory. On the other hand the problem is too urgent to be set aside until psychology can give unequivocal answers to the questions put to it. The situation is similar to that facing Justice in any criminal court: rarely can evidence be sufficient to satisfy the criteria of the laboratory, but *some* decision must be reached. The scientist can say that he has insufficient evidence and be prepared to wait for generations before he secures it, while the court has to make what is—from the scientist's point of view—a guess. In the light of this analogy it seems that the statesman, and the electors he represents, have to make up their minds on psychological problems, while the psychologists, as such, refuse to reach conclusions, and to make matters worse the politically minded rarely have any psychological training. It is with the hope that some small assistance may be given in making good the latter deficiency that this essay is offered. It is an attempt to show how *one* psychologist would approach some current problems and reach conclusions that are, scientifically, only highly tentative hypotheses and should not be taken as representing either established theory or even the speculative views of most psychologists. As a scientist I should publish nothing unless it were an incomplete analysis but this would be too dull to stimulate thought in any but other psychologists. So predictions are risked—based on psychological reasoning but with insufficient data—simply because it is these conclusions that are likely to provoke the thought, and the kind of thinking, that is so vitally needed to-day.

J. T. M.

15 *July* 1944

CHAPTER I

THE *HERRENVOLK* MYTH AND ITS CONSEQUENCES

'This war will not see victors or vanquished, but only survivors and annihilated' (HITLER).

'Before destruction can compass the heart of our nation we shall turn this Fortress of Europe into a whirlpool, a fatal suction, the roar of which will blot out everything except the cry for blood' (*Front und Heimat*, 13 July 1944).

ANALOGIES BETWEEN THE GERMAN AND RUSSIAN SYSTEMS

There are two opinions frequently expressed about Russia; each is incompatible with the other and both are uncritical. The first states bluntly that the Nazi and Communist systems are essentially alike and equally menacing to the democratic world. The other argues from the hatred of the Communists for the Nazis that the former are 'democratic' and are in the van of the forces struggling for freedom and social betterment throughout the world. What the truth is history may eventually reveal, but the events studied by the future historian will have been determined in no small measure by what the democracies have conceived to be the truth. If public opinion is no more intelligent than to produce rival formulae such as those cited, that opinion will, so soon as Germany is defeated, shout either for military preparedness against Russia or for the remodelling of our constitutions on what are conceived to be Russian lines, or, most likely, for both at once. In the meantime, public opinion is being formed under the impact of events but still more by the interpretation put on events. It is, then, the object of this essay to make some suggestion as to what the ideologies of the National Socialists and Communists mean to Germans and to Russians and how the national trends symbolized in these political theories may affect the behaviour of the nationals.

One word should be said in answer to a possible criticism. It may be objected that the ideologies of dictator countries are mere hand-outs to the robots whose actions are governed by the edicts of their rulers: the fate of the people is determined by the policy of the dictator. Such statements are merely less inaccurate for dictatorships than for democracies, but that does not make them unqualifiedly true. In the first place, every people that enjoy any unity at all have a common ethos; similar Weltanschauung, no matter how vague, and similar ways of behaving in emergencies. If a policy is forced on them that does not fit their ethos, they may accept it supinely, but they will not fight and die for it. Italy is an excellent example of this, for neither regimentation of opinion nor aggressive imperialism belongs to the Italian character. So eventual collapse of Fascism was psychologically predictable. But, at the same time, this example teaches us how long-term such predictions have to be. A sufficiently dominant ruler may keep an artificial system going for such a long time as to make it appear as if the State really was his creature. Indeed it seems as if prediction as to immediate action should be based on the character of the ruler, while remote behaviour should be assigned to the national character. The psychologist has available for his study the institutions and history of a people, but he rarely if ever can learn the data on which knowledge of a personality must be based. Consequently the psychologist can seldom make valid short-term predictions; but he should, in theory at least, be able to make a good guess as to how the trends of national behaviour will work themselves out. Secondly, it is doubtful if dictators ever make up ideologies in which they themselves do not believe. When we hear a man we consider a gangster handing out political theory we think to be nonsense, we are prone to assume that he has made it up to fool or placate the multitude. But it is difficult to lie consistently and to act up to one's lie, while it is all too easy to be deluded and sincere. We should make fewer mistakes in our judgments about our enemies if we always assumed them sincere until proved to be lying, when they express opinions that in our mouths would be lies.

The following similarities between the present German and Russian systems of organization are so familiar as to need little more than a bare mention. In each country there is a pyramiding system of authority culminating in the dictatorship of the leader of a one-party government. The Party is a minority composed of those ideologically sound, of proved efficiency in leadership, recruited (in theory) without regard to birth or fortune and specially trained for leadership from childhood. Other opinion is suppressed by liquidation of those who hold it and, particularly for the discovery of dissidence, secret police are freely used. The party leaders have been aptly called 'priests of a religion of this world'.

Both ideologies have indeed a number of features which are characteristic of religion rather than of political theory:

(1) Orthodoxy is held to be essential and no compromise is permitted.

(2) There are supernatural powers resident in the faith. Inspiration coming from belief in the system is not explained psychologically; its results are treated quite frankly as miraculous. In Germany, this superhuman power is ascribed to the Führer, the Führerprinzip,* or at times just to National Socialism. In Russia the 'people' or the 'proletariat' works the miracle, but 'people' refers to workers communistically organized, not to one race. In both countries achievements under the regime are never ascribed solely to natural and psychological forces but are hailed as accomplishments that could never have been achieved except for the magic of the 'system'.

(3) Knowledge of the ideology is not held to be inborn but is inculcated by education. Belief in the value of this indoctrination is shown in the time spent on it in both countries even during training for technical work, and during the season of stress when man-hours are precious. When time is short the

* See p. 66.

technical education is curtailed but not the ideo-
logical.

(4) 'Truth' does not come through revelation but
by instruction, that is, propaganda, on which there
is a reliance that is incredible to anyone brought up
in a democratic country. Essentially the system of
propaganda is that developed centuries ago by Rome.
It consists at once of censorship and positive indoctrination, particularly of the young. (We may
compare here the insistence in this country by religious sects on the right to have separate religious
instruction in schools.)

(5) Just as in all religions, Divine Law is held to
be superior to human obligations, so in Germany and
Russia, crimes against the State are considered to be
more serious than infringement of any individual
'rights', and loyalty to the State must override obligations to parent, spouse or friend.

An obvious contrast appears in economic theory,
but the evolutions in both countries have tended
towards similarity in this field. National Socialism
avowed the policy of maintaining individual property rights and the capitalistic ordering of production. In practice, however, and particularly in
preparation for and the prosecution of war, the
tendency has been more and more towards state
ownership of, as well as regulation of, production.
Communism began in almost literal form but has
allowed a profit motive to develop in wage-earning,
distribution, prospecting for mines, etc. Even the
inheritance of money is now allowed in the form of

some government loans at least. So far, however, the Kremlin has not compromised on the basic principle of State control of the means of production in industry. On the whole, however, Stalin's brand of communism has resulted in what is really a national socialism.

The economic and governmental differences between Germany and Russia are, apparently, no greater than those between Britain and the United States. Why then have the Germans such a terror of 'Bolshevism'? The answer would seem to be that similar systems have been implanted on different soil, on countries with markedly different history and traditions.

THE ORIGIN OF GERMAN PREDATORY POLICY AND ITS DELUSIONAL DEVELOPMENT

The most fundamental differences are geographic and ethnic. Germany is a relatively small country in the middle of Europe with a population speaking the same language, and sufficiently similar in physical type for their people to have developed and accepted the view that they compose a single race. Within the narrow confines of Europe no people can greatly increase its wealth merely by intensive exploitation of its natural resources. The traditional method of aggrandizement is conquest. At the time when colonists from other European states were over-running the uncivilized parts of the world overseas, Germany was engaged in the process of coming into

being as a union of many small states. By the time
that the union had become effective, there were no
longer available any large empty spaces in the world
for Germany to overrun. They had not lost in the
race; they had never really entered for it until it was
too late. Whereas other countries, particularly Great
Britain, could dispose of their surplus population by
migration to countries under their own flags, the
Germans could migrate only with the loss of their
nationality. Manifestly more efficient than their
neighbours in many respects, as a nation they could
not expand. Reich-consciousness came into being at
the very time when imperialism was in fashion and
there was no empire to have—except by conquest.

Thus Germany was faced by the alternatives of
remaining a relatively small country—and probably
breaking up again into its smaller parts—or of using
its united power in wars of expansion. In the latter
case a moral justification had to be found for what
was a crudely predatory programme. This necessity
arose from two sources. First, only the Prussians
were really bellicose by tradition and the other com-
ponent states had to be persuaded of the necessity
for war. Second, Germans had not lived long enough
in a segregated community with its own conventions
and moral standards to consider theirs as the only,
and the ultimate, ethical system. They were not
isolationists but vividly aware of foreign opinion,
hence their compulsive tendency to find some moral
argument in support of every action. (The Japanese
never trouble themselves to justify Pearl Harbour;

but the Germans have had wearisome explanations for every infraction of international laws or agreements.) So, *pari passu* with the rise of imperialism, came the development of the *Herrenvolk* myth. If the Germans were a chosen people, the authors and defenders of European culture, it was also their duty to be its missionaries, or, rather, to be its administrators, for, once the idea of racial superiority or inferiority became essential in their Weltanschauung, it was inevitable that Utopia would be a world in which the Herrenvolk ruled, while all others should serve as Providence had intended them to.

Similar ideas are probably implicit in the attitude of any powerful nation, but they remain unexpressed, or, if put into words, are likely to cause derision—that kind of chauvinism is out of date. Moreover in the structure of a nation's attitude there are usually other, and countervailing, latent ideas. This is analogous to the mixture of unconscious motives in an individual, which, through combination and compromise, eventuate in the conscious personality. In the individual, when unconscious ideas come to conscious expression in their original form, they produce mental symptoms. Something similar seems to have happened in Germany. When extremists in the 19th and early 20th centuries formulated the tribal god and Herrenvolk myth, they were not laughed at. But neither were their ideas incorporated into a set political theory. However they were allowed currency and the logical extensions of them resulted in a Weltanschauung that was delusional in type. *If the* mission of Germany was to conquer the world, this 'fact' would be as apparent to the world as it was to Germans. Unless the statesmen of foreign countries were complete fools, they would, if at all realistic, prevent German expansion before it was too late. Thus arose the delusion of encirclement. It was quite logical, if one accepted the original premiss and, as with all such delusions, it was not difficult to find a proof for it by an appropriate selection of data. Thus came 1914. To the Allies, the German motive for waging war was purely predatory; some Germans probably were consciously inspired by that motive and it was probably operative with the majority although not honestly avowed. But it seems that in addition practically everyone believed that the Kaiser's Reich was threatened with annihilation at the hands of jealous neighbours.

Actually in 1914, Germans seemed to be in a fair way towards gaining economic and financial control of the world. Why were they not satisfied with this? Since they were patently winning a peaceful pre-eminence, why should they seek a military one? There seems to be only one answer to this and that is an 'inferiority complex'. Ultimately this might be traced to roots far back in German history—the loss of their best blood in the Thirty Years' War and so on. But there was ample basis for it in current ideology. The patient who suffers from an inferiority complex is not actually inferior in comparison with his fellows, but he feels himself to be so because, unconsciously, he has set himself a goal that he actually is incapable of achieving. Anything that he actually accomplishes seems puny in comparison with his secret ambition, his hidden delusion of greatness. He is as greedy for praise as he is dissatisfied with himself. Nothing but public acclaim of him as a superman could make his unconscious fantasy a reality. Nothing but a world-wide acknowledgment of German supremacy could make the Teutons into a real Herrenvolk. It is also arguable that the persistent and ruthless persecution of the Jews represents a compulsive effort by the German people to cauterize away their own inferiority.

EMERGENCE OF THE NATIONAL SOCIALIST PARTY

But in 1918, Germany lost the war. What was going to happen to the paranoid Weltanschauung? The *raison d'être* of Hohenzollern Germany was conquest; if that ambition were abandoned economic necessity would be all that remained to bind the states together, Germany's soul would be lost, and, without a vision, the people would perish. It seemed at first that the Weimar constitution furnished insufficient inspiration and that the country was dying. Dispirited by military defeat, it was all too easy to see in reparations a confirmation of earlier fears; the Allies' fingers were about Germany's throat and slowly throttling her. Why struggle? Why sacrifice oneself to save a moribund state? Dissolution was the logical outcome of 1918, but the war-weary victors funked the responsibilities which that judgment entailed. It was easier to let the company drift into ruin than to declare it bankrupt, wind up its affairs, and let the shareholders have what assets would remain.

But there were others in addition to the Olympians at Versailles who refused to read the writing on the wall. These were Germans, patriots from their point of view, but, from ours, a group madder than any Junkers, who were to become the National Socialist Party. Some were idealists, some careerists and some just hooligans. Together they worked out an ideology and a programme that offered equal opportunity for devotion, ambition and brutality. The correlation of such apparent incompatibles is possible only in a group that is both intellectually and morally self-sufficient—the very essence of insanity, when it is an individual who becomes a law unto himself. The most unreal element in the earlier German ideology—the Herrenvolk myth—was placed in the foreground. (In 1914 and the years preceding it Germany's duty of overrunning the world was based on its *Kultur*, which was too efficient to be laughed away as pure lunacy. *Kultur* was probably only a symbolic expression for the Herrenvolk idea; at least it disappeared when the latter claim was made with crude directness by the Nazis.) Being quasi-divine the Germans could treat all other peoples as inferior species: one castrates a horse in order to make it docile, beats it when it refuses to work and feeds it only in order that it may be able to work; one does not make promises to a horse and feel any compunction about breaking them. Coupled with the superman idea was a crude materialism. The superiority of the German was essentially in all the assets of a warrior: strength, hardihood and hardness, courage, discipline and good weapons. So force was both extolled and made a standard of comparison, this being justified on pseudo-biological grounds by a narrow interpretation of the doctrine of the survival of the fittest. People who welcomed the arbitrament of arms were good Germans; those who preferred to compete in other fields were just 'the lesser breeds without the law'. This theory has had two important developments.

ANTISEMITISM

On the face of it Germans had been proved to be not stronger but weaker than the rest of the world in 1918. But if it could be proved that the warriors had not been defeated in the field but tricked into surrender, then the doctrine of the Herrenvolk could be maintained. And this was 'proved' by the simple logic of the bully. The betrayers of Germany were civilians, politicians who listened to the wiles of enemy propaganda: they were 'intellectuals', pacifists, internationalists, who could not be good Nordics (if Nordics were by definition primarily fighters). These were the people who came to the top under the Weimar Republic and were typified by the Jews. It was easy to represent the struggle of the

Nazis for power as a conflict between Aryan and non-Aryan. By beating up Jews and the soft-hearted sympathizers with Jews, the Nazis proved that might was right and that Nordics—the real Germans—were God's chosen people. Q.e.f. became q.e.d. But the matter did not end there. Under the Kaiser an inferiority reaction had produced the encirclement myth. The allegedly unconquerable force of German arms had failed to break the ring of hostile powers. This was a fact of history which could not be gainsaid. But there had not been a fight to the finish. This had been prevented by the Jews. So—developed chiefly during the last couple of years—has come the lunatic theory that the enemies of the Third Reich are not really the British, the Americans, perhaps not even the 'sub-human' Russians, but the Jews who invented both plutocracy and Bolshevism. To the German people is held out the hope that the Allies will realize the disintegrating policy of the Jews and liquidate them as the Germans have done and then, of course, make peace. Thus, instead of being beleaguered by military powers, the encirclement of Nazi Germany is due to the wiles of the devil, whose other name is Jewry.

THE NIHILISTIC TREND

The other development of Herrenvolk-force-worship may explain why Germany, in defiance of precedent, goes on fighting an obviously losing battle, but at the same time the explanation conjures up a terrifying vision of Central Europe at the end of the war. Although they may be individually sane, the National Socialist Party leaders make up a group that is inspired by what is, essentially, a delusional system. To this they are devoted not only by conviction but also by necessity; they have made their bed and must lie on it, for there is no longer any other available to them. In this naughty world force is a necessary implement of defence and for the punishment of wickedness and vice, but it is at best destructive. So it runs counter to all the constructive trends in society. If force is elevated and made an end in itself, it inevitably depreciates all other values and becomes nihilistic. This perversion is, of course, regressive, and National Socialism has been from the beginning implicitly antagonistic to the moral and aesthetic values that have been slowly evolved in European civilization. The Nazis were going to dominate by destruction or to destroy and thus dominate. The obverse and reverse of the same coin. They began by destroying the old Germany, went on to subjugate the even more defenceless small countries within easy reach, and then challenged civilization itself. But, if the legions of the world are too much for them, what can they then do? The answer is easy: go on destroying what is destructible until nothing within the range of their power is left. This is the meaning of the daily repeated slogans, 'The greatest victory or the greatest defeat in history', 'Complete victory or complete annihilation', and so on—there are many variations of this inevitable antithesis. So, within the limits of

their power, the satellite and occupied countries will
be gutted but Germany will still be left. Then it, too,
must be destroyed. No one must be able to say that
the Nazis faltered in their crusade. History will be
able to record a novelty—a country that fought until
it ceased to exist.

THE GREAT STRATEGIC ERROR

Nazi ideology not only made the present war inevitable, it has also contributed largely to basic errors
in German strategy. National Socialism as a system
of government might be exportable, other peoples
might be converted to it by missionary efforts. But,
if German superiority is resident not in political
theory but in German blood, then no other people
could adopt it. Export of National Socialism that is
linked with the Herrenvolk theory could have been
accomplished only by the migration of Germans who
dispossessed foreign populations, exterminating or
enslaving them. If the peoples who have been the
victims of this policy had never known freedom they
might have accepted a change of masters, but, as they
are loyal to their government or are liberty-loving,
they bow their necks to the yoke only when the task-
master is present. It has thus followed that military
victory and successful exploitation of enemy labour
have proved to be quite different problems. An army
sufficient to conquer an opponent's army can overrun
his territory but a similar man-power may be needed
to maintain its profitable occupation. Germany is

now paying the price for having bitten off more than she could chew. The dragon has been slain but its teeth have grown into partisans. How this mistake came to be made is psychologically explicable. Three factors cooperated to produce it.

The first was overvaluation of military power: dramatic conquests produced the feeling of omnipotence. An army, that could almost effortlessly destroy the armed forces of, say, Poland, would surely be able to control the unarmed populace. And so it could, were it used. But in German planning the mere *threat* of the Wehrmacht was to take the place of the conquering soldiery, a handful of whom could make examples of recalcitrant Poles. Knowing that any given rebel could be easily destroyed, the Poles were expected to bow before this threatened force as helplessly as they would have to do were it physically exercised. The expectation that a sword could be used as a magician's wand rested, probably, on a second factor. Acceptance of a threat of force as an equivalent to actual force was a phenomenon with which the Nazis were familiar at home. Paradoxically the docility of Germans contributed largely to the belief that Teutons were a Herrenvolk through the illogical sequence: the Nazis have proved the invincibility of force within the Reich, the force of the Nazis is the same as German might, so Germans are invincible. The third factor was belief in propaganda. The Nazis had come to power not only by violence but also by exploiting the magic of propaganda. This propaganda was not based on general scientific principles but was an empirical rule of thumb: Repeat often enough what you want to have believed and the listeners will eventually believe it. There is a limited truth in this formula, but the Nazis forgot when ascribing their results to this barrage type of propaganda that other factors contributed to their success. Two important ones were the work of the Gestapo and the censorship which prevented the German victim from hearing anything but their own side of the story. The foreigner who is familiar with other arguments and countervailing facts is prone to be simply bored with what he calls 'just propaganda'. But, the Nazis thought, methods that worked with Germans would work with other peoples as well. So, if there were any among the population of the occupied territories who were not cowed by the whip, they could be seduced by propaganda into believing that slavery was beneficial.

GERMAN SUPERIORITY A PHYSICAL INHERITANCE

It will be seen that what is wrong with the German Herrenvolk idea is its materialism, its concentration on a racial superiority, on the blood that is transmitted by heredity. It is not a culture that could be shared by anyone who chose to acquire it, so its dispersal must depend on the migration of those who inherit the godlike blood. Conceivably a sufficiently virile stock might in time overrun the world, but it would have to be a slow process with annihilation of the indigenous inhabitants in any conquered territory followed by an exploitation of its natural resources before further excursions were made. A Herrenvolk theory where the folk are those who avow the superiority of their culture rather than of their race leads to different behaviour. They may conquer with the sword but they welcome as partners all who adopt their political, social and moral systems. Such a culture can spread as does a religion—to which, indeed, it is psychologically akin.

WHOLESALE DESTRUCTION AS A GOAL

No one can know better than do the leaders in Germany to-day that their programme of world domination is now hopeless. Then why go on fighting? Those who defend moral and spiritual causes may prefer death to renunciation of their faith and they may believe that, by death, the martyr may achieve that which his mortal powers were unable to accomplish. But this is because his faith is centred on something that is immaterial. If reliance is placed on physical superiority and so soon as it is seen that that force is insufficient for its task, the rational policy is to conserve it, to shield it from assault while it is weak, and to build it up again so that one can eventually strike again on better terms. Thus the High Command counselled peace in 1918. If the German General Staff had the power to-day that it wielded before and during the last war an armistice—on almost any terms—would probably have been sought long since. But one of the primary objectives of the Nazis on coming into power was to secure control over the Wehrmacht. This they attained and then maintained, probably following the Russian model, by infiltrating the Services with S.S. personnel, the German equivalent of Political Commissars. The fate of the armed forces as of the civilians is now in the hands of the Party. Its leaders, zealots for destruction, can pull down the pillars of their temple and leave not one stone standing on another. Thus they can not only rob their enemies of the fruits of victory, but leave to them as legacy a festering sore where once was the 'home of European civilization'.

For the accomplishment of this apocalyptic triumph it is only necessary that the war should go on, for the Allied Nations will perform the destruction in Central Europe that German arms are unable to complete in its periphery. So all forces, both material and moral, are mobilized for the maintenance of the struggle, although the lure of victory is being more and more neglected in German propaganda. Defeatist talk is punished with exemplary ferocity when the Gestapo overhears it and, although the numbers of secret police in the Heimat may be greatly reduced, their ubiquity is now so firm a tradition that the memory of it suffices to curb public manifestation of disaffection and, of course, inhibits the effective organisation of any peace movement. Secondly all possible material resources are ruthlessly mobilized, no matter what impoverishment in the future that may entail. For instance there is the scrapping of plants for the manufacture of consumers' goods, which means that, in so far as the orders are carried out, factories will not be able to turn swords into ploughshares when peace does come. Again, this year's supplies of chemical fertilizers is 51 per cent of the pre-war distribution. (In this country there is an increase up to as much as fourfold in some localities.) This will mean an inevitable drop in the 1944 harvest—perhaps a catastrophic one, which, taken with the loss of territory in the East, must mean severe cuts into the already marginal rations. The Nazi authorities must be aware of these trends, they must know that if we cannot be forced next winter to feed and clothe their countrymen they will perish. Once victory is impossible continuation of the war only makes utter ruin the more certain: 'Non-capitulation' is a cover for a policy of national destruction that must be every day a more deliberate one.

THE COURSE OF PROPAGANDA

But, of course, the Party attitude towards the outcome of the war is displayed most clearly in its propaganda. The leitmotif is 'No compromise peace is possible'. When it became evident that advance into Russia was not just a triumphal procession, the spectre of a possible defeat not unnaturally appeared and was exploited in propaganda which emphasized the bestiality and cruelty of the Bolshevik 'sub-humans', who would lay waste the Reich were they not themselves first destroyed. The remoteness and foreignness of Russians made the propagandist's task easy. Superstitious terror was added to the natural fear of reprisal for barbarities inflicted on them by the Herrenvolk. Germans were easily persuaded that the issue in the East was the starkly simple alternative of victory or annihilation. But as confidence in victory began to weaken another possibility was mooted: the British who were 'gentlemen', and later the British and Americans, might overrun the Reich before the eastern hordes broke in. Although this would be a sorry awakening from the dreams of conquest, it was a prospect the average German could face without terror. To the Nazis, however, it meant their end not merely as individuals but also as the representatives of the Herrenvolk creed. So both expedience and faith necessitated an onslaught on this dangerous compromise hope. Thus the 'Strength through Fear' propaganda began. At first Goebbels and his minions had an uphill task: respect for the British—although they might be hated—was too strong a tradition to be broken by what was obviously 'just propaganda'. But then came the accentuation of R.A.F. attacks on Germany in the spring of 1942. To treat them as negligible was no longer feasible, so an entirely new line was started— perhaps the soundest programme psychologically of any the Germans have initiated: Being unable to accomplish results of any direct military significance, the R.A.F. had turned on the civilian population and was trying to break its nerve. Bombs were weapons used by cowards who would not fight fair, but, if civilians refused to break under the strain, then the British strategy would be defeated. Instead of maintaining the ever more ridiculous attempt to deny the reality of heavy raids, destruction (provided it was only of civilian property) could not only be admitted, but its horror could also be exploited. Undoubtedly the labelling of R.A.F. attacks as 'Terrorangriffe' has been effective in bolstering morale on the Home Front, but it has proved equally useful in supporting the strength-through-fear programme.

The proof of the pudding is in the eating. In other words, conviction is based on actual experience rather than on instruction and argument. Even the docile German was likely to remain unmoved by a purely verbal claim that the democracies were inspired by ruthless lust to destroy not merely the Nazi government, but the men, women and children of Germany, to wipe Germany off the map of Europe and to remove German culture from the pages of future history. But, when their government said this and then the R.A.F. and American airmen bombed churches, hospitals and museums, burned houses by thousands and slew innocent civilians by tens of thousands, who was to be believed? When the B.B.C. talked about 'military objectives' was it not the enemy who was indulging in pure propaganda? (We must remember that news has been so handled in Germany as to make it difficult for any German to realize that it was the Luftwaffe that began the bombing of civilians.) Then came 'unconditional surrender'. What does that mean? The democracies had some long-winded interpretation to the effect that Axis submission must be so complete as to symbolize military defeat. German propaganda said it meant turning over the country to men who liked killing women and children, who avowed the policy of taking forced labour to Siberia and so on. The Badoglio government surrendered unconditionally and that part of Italy then coming under Allied occupation suffered from looting, famine and disease, while the Italians who fought on in the north were in a much better case—according to the news that reached the Germans. The average German to-day may well say to himself, 'If I put all prejudices on one side, does it not look as if the democracies had sunk to the level of the brutal Russians? At any rate, I cannot surrender all by myself and, if I talked about sit down strikes, I should only be shot by the Gestapo. Is there anything I can do except just to carry on and perhaps some miracle may happen?'

MORALE IN DIFFERENT GERMAN GROUPS

Some such statement may approximate to the attitude of the average German civilian to-day but it is, perhaps, a mistake to formulate it so concisely. Long hours of routine work, no play and insufficient sleep do not promote the exercise of intellectual faculties. But there is also a specific factor operating to inhibit thought in the bombed areas at least. Protracted exposure to danger against which no effective measures can be taken is likely to produce apathy: panic, i.e.

a blind impulse to escape, may be an initial dramatic response to danger but, with continued repetition of the threat, even the capacity for fear seems to be exhausted. The inhabitants of much-bombed German cities seem, many of them, to have covered themselves with this protective cloak of insensibility. They are too numbed to think, and respond in an animal-like way to the immediate stimulus. They are like galley slaves who keep pulling at the oars because, if they pause for a moment, down comes the whip; but they have ceased to care whether the galley is pursuing a treasure ship or running from a man-of-war.

Another group is probably represented more largely in the armed forces and, there, particularly among those whose memories do not properly compass the days before the Third Reich. The only Germany they have known has been devoted to the worship and service of Thor; their knowledge of the rest of the world has been supplied by the Propaganda Ministry. They are not equipped to live in a normal world and to them 'victory or annihilation' is a fully satisfying formula. Victory is of course preferable, but a hero's death is also glorious. To be identified with the greatest conquest of history is inspiring, but to share in an apocalyptic end of all civilization is to participate in a mystical triumph. They are the natural heirs to the pessimistic philosophers whose lineage runs through so many German generations, and they are equally fertile soil for the morbid preoccupation with disaster which keeps recurring in Nazi propaganda and was best exemplified in the 'Stalingrad sacrifice' theme. These young warriors have no fear of death, but only of ceasing to be 'hard'. Provided they keep on fighting they will either be overlords in a Nazi world or translated to Valhalla. So long as there are enough of them to fight rearguard actions a definitive victory for Allied arms will be delayed and, indeed, the way in which the war will end will depend on the numbers of such stubborn troops as are available. If the advance of the Allied armies is sufficiently slow a German internal collapse will occur before the Wehrmacht is rendered impotent.

HOPE OF MIRACLES

Although the well-informed Nazi leaders may know that the game is up and be turning ever more towards a conscious policy of wholesale destructiveness, they cannot admit either their knowledge or the policy it engenders—perhaps not even to themselves. So their propaganda has to hold some carrot before the donkey's nose. The ominous military situation, destruction from bombing and the shortages patent to all, are good material for strength-through-fear and victory-or-annihilation propaganda, but by themselves would tend to suggest acceptance of the inevitable rather than continuation of the struggle. Some rationalization for the call to fight on must be given, but the best that can be fabricated is hardly rational, for it is a miracle. The people are told that, if they toil and suffer unfalteringly, victory will come supernaturally. What fate will produce is variously represented in a series of suggestions, none of which has been given a consistent and persistent publicity—a fact that reveals how half-hearted the sorely beset Propaganda Ministry is in promulgating this theme. Among the forms which the miracle assumes are the following: secret weapons which are openly spoken of in vague terms and the more specific nature of which has been suggested in well-planted rumours; large hidden reserves of men and materials; rivalry and quarrels between the Allies; imminent collapse in Russia as a result of exhaustion; social, economic and political breakdown in Great Britain that is presaged by widespread strikes; the possession by Germany of a trump card in the form of 'superior political weapons', which is perhaps intended to suggest that in the enemy countries all domestic or inter-Allied frictions are fomented by German agents. Then there is the recurrent emphasis on the mystical power of the National Socialist system which is treated as being frankly supernatural. German will-power can more than compensate for her deficiencies in men and material, even for relative inferiority in scientific devices. Particularly at the time of Hitler's birthday the 'magic of the Führerprinzip' was invoked by Goebbels and others. *Das Schwarze Korps* said: 'Take away the spiritual forces which Hitler signifies and cut the ties of faith linking us all to him personally, and what remains? Only men able to do what is human, to endure only what is human and who will one day yield to what is all too human.'

DISINTEGRATION

Thus the stage is set for an exhaustion of the Reich far greater than that in 1918 and, if its present rulers are covertly working for *Weltuntergang*, for an 'end of the world', they are better equipped than any of their predecessors for its accomplishment. Indeed for the undoing of Germany they may be working better than they know. As exhaustion of man-power, munitions, machines, consumer goods and food proceeds, the distribution, allocation and exploitation of what there is become ever greater problems, demanding more resource and more energy. Ultimately a time comes when mere courage and endurance are not enough. The more elaborate an organization is, the more imagination is required to keep it elastic. Weary officials will not have that adaptability. When a breakdown comes it is likely to be rapidly cumulative. Should this collapse occur before the Allied armies are in occupation and able to supervise the country's economy, an appalling chaos is likely. Millions of foreigners will be roaming the country, trying to make their way home and living by larceny and brigandage. The higher officials will be fleeing from Allied vengeance and from their compatriots who seek to pay off old scores; the exiguous food supplies which can be made to cover minimum needs by careful distribution will be concentrated in the hands of looters and black market operators, so famine will result; finally, the sanitary services will inevitably fail and pestilence assume unprecedented proportions. In a word, it will be chaos, a chaos such as no occupied country has known or is likely to know for the simple reason that a highly organized nation, whose existence depended on that organization, will have lost its government and not got another. In no other country have *all* those capable of exercising authority been liquidated or else concentrated in a Party that will be wiped out when the débâcle comes.

If this prognosis is at all justified, discussions as to how Germany is to be restrained from fomenting another war are academic in the extreme. The problem will not be the prevention of German military resurgence, but rather the reorganization of a Central Europe from which Germany has disappeared. An area in the middle of Europe peopled by isolated peasants and roaming bands of brigands would become an export centre for pestilence, both actual and moral, endangering not merely the continent but the whole world. This corruption could be prevented only if German territory were given priority in rehabilitation, which is highly improbable.

CHAPTER II

THE RUSSIAN IDEOLOGY AND ITS EVOLUTION

Since it is fantastically improbable that anything we say or do at the moment could affect the Russian will to fight, any study of the Weltanschauung of the Soviets might seem inopportune. But that is to take a short view. There are two reasons at least why we should concern ourselves with it. If we privately hold the view—as some may—that Bolshevism is almost as great a menace as National Socialism, then our moral support for our Allies may lack the conviction which makes effort persistent and effective. Secondly, the politics of war do not suddenly change to those of peace. One merges slowly into the other and if the earlier and later policies are at variance there is certain to be an intermediate stage reeking of insincerity. Frank criticism produces less friction between individuals than does hostility poorly cloaked by words of friendship. At the moment the relations between this country and Russia are friendly, if only because we are co-belligerents. When peace comes that attitude will be maintained officially for some time, even although there may be unofficial and private misgiving. In the long run, however, friendly relations will depend chiefly on Russian behaviour, i.e. whether the Kremlin does or does not pursue a live-and-let-live policy. If it becomes aggressive, interferes with our internal affairs, or stands in the way of our meeting our treaty obligations, then friction will be inevitable. This possibility—a probability according to the opinion of many private citizens who are not without influence —forces on us a long-term problem. If we assume that friendship will be permanent but have eventually to change our tune, there will be an inconsistency detrimental to our prestige. If we make that assumption, while fearing it is misguided, and try to make it an actuality with stentorian protestations of our faith, the inconsistency will be all the more glaring. On the other hand, if we assume that friction is ultimately probable or inevitable, we can be judiciously guarded, sacrificing temporary advantage for the sake of the consistency which fortifies policy and commands respect for it.

CONTINUITY IN RUSSIAN HISTORY

It is thus highly desirable to see what the evolution of Russian foreign policy is likely to be. But have we any data that can be used as a basis even for a guess? Tsarist Russia that lived long enough to develop some definite trend is dead; a revolution, it is said, has swept away the old regime, and we have only the history of the past quarter of a century on which to base a judgment as to the future of the U.S.S.R. What seems to make the problem more difficult is the apparent fluidity of Bolshevik policy, both domestic and foreign, during the past twenty-five years. But if one neglects the superficial, formal meanings of the terms used to denominate institutions and objectives, and tries to discover what the drift of the Russian experiment is, then it appears that there is continuity in Russian history, that where the Communist pro- gramme has run counter to human nature in general or to Russian nature in particular, it has lapsed, and that, as the graft grows, it seems to partake more and more of the nature of the tree whose stem it has joined. The events of a revolution may be catastrophic for individuals, but the traditions of the survivors are symbolized in new titles and new catchwords. A craftsman may tackle a new job with old tools or he may try to do an old job with new tools; but he cannot begin from scratch.

The doctrinaire Marxists who effected the revolu- tion apparently thought they could recreate not only Russia but the whole world; experience, however, has made them less ambitious. Officially the Third International has been abandoned. (The suspicious say this is only a blind, but this is a problem to be dis- cussed later.) So far as internal polity is concerned, the reappearance of what was fundamentally Russian has been more extensive than its abolition. The classes were abolished by the simple expedient of liquidating the gentry, the Tsarist officials and the bourgeoisie. But they have been recreated. In fact, if 'aristocracy' means legally guaranteed privileges to certain classes, then there is much more of it in Russia than in Britain. True, it has no hereditary rights but, even if one assumes that development to be inevitable, one could hardly expect it to begin with the first generation of the new nobility. The revolutionary government could not get along without money and its possession personally by individuals. 'Capitalism' is to the Soviets what racial impurity is to the National Socialist state, but in practice so long as a German is not coloured or a Jew he can be a good Nazi, while in the U.S.S.R. the machinery of capitalism is used freely and the difference between the economy of the Socialist Republics and that of the capitalistic states is merely the extent to which government supervision is direct and centrally planned. Workers in Russia are more controlled by management than under frank capitalism, and reduction of wages can lead to increased financial reward to the managers. Undoubtedly, however, it is still more difficult for a Russian to live merely upon dividends and interest than elsewhere in the world, but the narrow end of this wedge is visible. Government is centred in an autocrat as in the old days, and the administration is in the hands of a bureaucracy, both more efficient and less corruptible than its Tsarist prototype, but still a bureaucracy responsible not to the people but to the autocrat. Religion was banned but, in its formal aspect, lived underground and has now been allowed a public existence, while some of the peculiar attributes of Orthodoxy have been transferred to politics.

ADAPTATION OF THEORETIC COMMUNISM
TO REALITIES

In such respects National Socialism and Bolshevism
are in marked contrast. The former reeks of the
pathological with its regression to the primitive and
its uncompromising conquer-or-die programme. But
Russia seems to shed its irrationalities as it goes on
and to become more realistic every day. Its incon-
sistencies are not those of the psychopath but of the
highly educable adolescent who can drop his follies
as he gains experience. If we wish to frame a policy
vis-a-vis post-war Russia, we must not focus our
attention on its early objectives nor on the shibbo-
leths that survived from that period, we should not
even concentrate on present behaviour, but we should
try to discern what the evolutionary *process* is whereby
ancient traditions are being integrated with socialist
objectives so as to produce something that is neither
one nor the other but really a new type of civilization.

When the Bolshevists came into power their programme was fantastically unpractical. Russia's
economy was shattered and its administration dis-
integrated. At the same time it was hoped to organize
a starving people in the interest of production
according to a system that had never existed except
in literature, while the surplus enthusiasm of the
people was to foment a world-wide revolt of the
proletariat. A state which had a soul but no body
had to incorporate itself by organizing the efforts
of its citizens somehow. In the all-important sphere

of economics, no one knew how to regulate production and distribution except by the old machinery of capitalism. So, with the country *in extremis*, Lenin bowed to the inevitable, threw overboard the ark of the covenant and allowed private enterprise to operate. Shipwreck was prevented, but private enterprise quickly grew in extent and, if unchecked, would probably have displaced the socialist system entirely. The anomalous character of Russia under the New Economic Policy was obvious. A large capitalist economy was in operation in order to keep alive a country whose *raison d'être* was said to be the abolition of capitalism throughout the world. If this process had gone on unchecked, disintegration would have been inevitable. Private enterprise, when it had displaced State enterprise completely, would not have tolerated the maintenance of the Marxian creed, by that time effete; it would abolish State control of production and distribution and might well turn Russia over again to foreign capitalists. Stalin saw this, saw that incompatible aims were being followed, that the country was defenceless militarily while the Nazis were rattling sabres in the West (although not yet in power). The Marxian experiment had already failed, so the thing to do was to start another one quickly, the experiment of a national socialism. On the one hand private enterprise was to be curbed and on the other hand the objective of the people's labours was to be made the U.S.S.R., a country to defend and a country to enrich.

But what was the country? Under Lenin there was an international ideal and a territory that had belonged to the Tsars. Stalin's task was to reawaken the loyalty that had been focussed on the Tsar and transfer it to an ideal of nationalism in the economic sphere, a development that could be incorporated, as it were, in the great Red Army and was to be implemented in the Five Year Plans under which the surplus of production went more to rearmament than to raising the standards of comfort. Continuity was achieved by keeping the term 'Communism', the salutation 'Comrade' and the catchword 'Rule of the proletariat', but the functioning idea was to be that of patriotism, loyalty to the New Russia. When Hitler invaded the soil of sacred Russia, Stalin's task was made easy. The old loyalties could be invoked without fear of this being called treason to the new regime. So, in the interest of fighting spirit, the memories of Tsarist military triumphs were awakened and the prowess of Tsarist generals extolled. Thus it is not merely in the field of religion that the links with Russia's past are being openly exploited. There is, however, no sign that this recognition of the past implies any likelihood of a reconstitution of Tsarist institutions. What we shall see, rather, is a union, wherever that is possible, of what was implicit in those institutions with compatible elements of the new doctrines. Revolutionary zeal sees to it that nothing from the past is revived or maintained out of veneration for tradition, while realism will go on pruning away from the Marxist programme everything that does not work either because it does not suit the Russian people or because it is economically inexpedient. The shape of things to come may therefore be glimpsed if we can identify the Muscovite in his Communist clothes and see to what extent the part he is playing is becoming natural to him.

THE MEANING OF 'CAPITALISM'

Every national ideology seems, like a religion, to have its God and its devil. These agencies, although they may have clear enough labels, are in practice invoked in such varied situations as to make it seem as if they were spiritual, mystical powers incorporating what the nation feels to be good or evil rather than just the political or economic principles indicated by their names. The good is both an ideal to serve and a power which can elevate the common man to a level of heroic achievement. The evil spirit is the God of one's enemies who does not fight fair but works through spies or inspires domestic treason. The name of a Soviet's god is the 'Proletariat' or 'The People'; the name of the devil is 'Capitalism'. Originally these rival spirits ruled or fought over the whole civilized world but now they have their geographically separated empires. The People rule in the U.S.S.R. while Capitalism, the Bolshevists aver, governs the rest of the world. Much history is involved in this statement and, if it be an accurate generalization, it carries profound implications for Russia's future.

SERF DISAFFECTION

The Russian peasant used to have the saying: 'The body belongs to the Tsar, the soul to God and the back to the Squire.' God, we may presume, was a fact of nature and to resent His proprietorship was as futile as to quarrel with gravity. The Tsar, too, who could turn the serf into a soldier by a stroke of his pen, was so distant a being as to be semi-divine, at least in his inaccessibility, but the Squire was a different matter. He was human and enjoyed no physical or obvious intellectual superiority proportionate to the share of this world's goods allotted to him. In what a man makes by his skill or the sweat of his brow he is bound to feel some kind of proprietary interest. He may cheerfully give it away to one who is an object of loyal devotion; but he is outraged if it is taken from him, particularly if he sees it ostentatiously squandered. Hence the peasants' revolts that had occurred sporadically for a couple of centuries at least and had always been suppressed physically, although spiritually resentment grew. Then came the abolition of serfdom and more disillusionment. As the peasants had to repay to the government the money that had bought their freedom they found themselves slaves to the government instead of slaves of the squires. Many migrated into industry, swelling the ranks of a proletariat that began in an earlier peonage. Their enemy was the *system* which prevented a man from enjoying the fruits of his labours. Heaven, or Utopia, was a place where there would be no such system, but it was not a place where there would be individual, intellectual, moral or spiritual liberty. (That is a kind of liberty that is sought by those who have already achieved some measure of economic security. 'Freedom' in our sense of the term is a luxury demanded only when the standard of living has risen above the level where mere subsistence is a matter of daily concern.) Inevitably there grew up a traditional hostility against a 'system' which made and maintained an economic servitude for the masses. Had there been, as exists in capitalistically organized countries, an opportunity for the exceptionally gifted to better themselves and become rulers rather than servants, development of class feeling might have been less intense. But the system offered few bribes to outstanding workers to leave their companions; instead it made them into agitators who translated feelings into words and made the labourer class-conscious.

Before a class can act effectively, no matter how numerous it is, it must be organized and it must know what it is fighting for: that is, it must have both leaders and an ideology, for organization and objective are interlocking factors. An illiterate proletariat whose members are worked close to the limits of physical endurance may mutter or may revolt locally and sporadically. But it can effect revolution only if it has leaders capable of formulating a programme and coordinating effort, which are tasks beyond the powers of those who have neither leisure nor education. The Russian proletariat left to itself might never have been able to cast off its shackles, but only by recalcitrance and sabotage to increase Russian inefficiency. Disaffection, however, was not confined to the lower classes. The 'intellectuals' of the middle and upper classes coveted the liberty of speech enjoyed in the West and were sympathetically horrified by the material plight of the working classes. Here were people who had the leisure and the education needed for planning and even the financial means to assist the occasional workers whose ability warranted their training as agitators. For generations their activities went on in spite of the omnipresence of the secret police. Many were the Utopias set up as goals, and many were the secret political societies that plotted at home and in exile for the attainment of these objectives. Eventually, however, it was the Bolsheviks' version of Marxism that had the numbers, the propaganda and the organization to carry the day after a displacement of Tsarism that was as much an internal disintegration as it was a revolution.

MARXISM AN IMPORTATION

Now it is important in considering the trend of Russian history to note that Marxian socialism was a product of the industrial capitalism of Western Europe, and not a product of Russian culture.

Russia was a predominantly agricultural, not industrial, country. Moreover, prior to 1917, industry, communications and economy in general were more under government ownership or control than in other 'capitalistic' countries and the finance of colonial expansion had been chiefly governmental. There was no strong industrial and mercantile class. This last is particularly important. Some observers have ascribed the defeat of Russia in the last war to the lack of a strong bourgeoisie. There were good generals and magnificent soldiers, but they were starved of supplies because production and distribution were managed by a totally inadequate number of civil servants and business men. Without the military failure the revolution would not have occurred at the time it did, although the volcano was bound to erupt sooner or later. But when it came it might not have been exploited by the Trotskys and the Lenins, exiles who were committed to formulae that reflected non-Russian conflicts, but it might have been engineered by patriots who offered remedies for the ills that were peculiarly Russian. Undoubtedly the belated Russian industrial revolution brought in its train some exploitation of the proletariat by private capitalists, but the trouble was older and deeper than that. It was a bureaucracy, subservient to an autocracy, that was reactionary because any fundamental reform seemed to threaten its absolutism. This system may have worked for the glory of Russia or for the prestige of the Tsar, but it neither represented, nor worked primarily for, the welfare of the people as a whole. That was what the people felt in their bones. Because 'capitalism' was only the name given to their enemy, its literal abolition was an impossibility and in many of its aspects it has been reinstated. But that name has complicated international relations as we shall see.

THE PRESENT POLITICAL CREED

The Russians now have a government that is as autocratic and bureaucratic as its predecessor. This is, indeed, the only form of administration which the people know and, probably, the only kind they want —for the present at least. But this government is no longer working for the safety and aggrandizement of an autocrat, of his family, or of an arbitrarily privileged class. It is working for the people as a whole; officials are the servants of the State, not its rulers; those who were slaves are now free, not individually but as a class. Working for the common good, individuals accept restrictions of personal liberty that were the signs and symbols of oppression when the apparent object of toil was the enrichment of the leisured class. The existence of privilege, too, is not resented because present-day privilege is the reward for outstanding service, because it has been earned and not inherited, and because what were once the trappings of nobility can now be displayed by one of the proletariat.

> He served—but served Polycrates—
> A Tyrant; but our tyrants then
> Were still, at least, our countrymen.

'The People' is a god who can give big rewards to
his faithful servants. Its priests—party officials—
issue orders that are final and supported by force, but
their spirit is 'mother knows best' and not an arbitrary 'father says'. Those who rebel are ungrateful
and not liberty-loving martyrs.

But, above all, 'The People' is a powerful god who
can create and fructify as can no other national or
political deity. Any revivalist can implant beliefs
in his audience, but enduring faith rests on the valida-
tion of experience, and any theory, if it is sufficiently
vague and general in scope, is being confirmed daily
in the experience of the uncritical. Every time we see
and hear the leaves of a tree rustle we know that the
wind is blowing. Every time the savage observes the
same phenomenon, he knows the spirit of the tree is
breathing and his breath is the wind. Everything
observable in Russia to-day that was not there in
Tsarist days—tractors, electrification, better schools
and hospitals, etc.—is a creation of Communism. For
generations the socialists had preached that all wealth
was the product of labour, and now a state composed
of nothing but 'workers' has not only reproduced
everything that the old regime could show but has
also created much that is totally new. If a community
can be sufficiently insulated from the rest of the world
by censorship, all that propaganda has to do is to
direct attention to the obvious in order to make its
case. If a peasant, who had never heard of a more
elaborate farming implement than a horse-drawn
plough, is given not only a tractor that pulls the

plough but a reaper and binder as well and is told that these are of Soviet manufacture, are they not the products of the creative power of Communism? Should a foreigner claim that they are but copies of American machines, he is laughed at as a teller of Münchausen tales. If Capitalism could produce such marvels, why were they not available in the Tsarist capitalistic days?

Incidentally, we have here an example of the practical superiority of Russian over German ideology. The Nazis boast of 'world power', but Communism already has its power demonstrable on every hand because it is obvious that no wealth is produced or military victory achieved without the work of the common man and the fighting of the common soldier. On the other hand, German world dominance has never in living memory been anything but a matter of faith and threats. One attempt to demonstrate it failed in 1918, and during the present war a second failure is tacitly admitted by the dropping of *Lebensraum* propaganda in favour of the war of defence. But not even a Russian defeat could disprove the claim that ultimate power rests in the hands of the proletariat.

'CAPITALISM' SYMBOLISES FOREIGN INFLUENCE

What is believed by the Communists to-day about their devil, 'Capitalism', is essential for an understanding of the attitude of the Soviets towards foreign

countries. The Russians are not professional econom-
ists and so can use the term 'capitalism' as a catchword
untroubled by the technical absurdity of its application to the system they overthrew and the political
ideals of the foreign countries which they believe to
be inimical. The exiles who engineered the revolution
gave the name of 'Capitalism' to the Tsarist regime,
and wished to exploit the unrest in Russia in the
interests of world-wide liberation of the proletariat.
But the vast bulk of the Russian workers were interested in the heaven on earth that Communism
would bring to their own land; they wanted peace for
recuperation and growth, not crusades for the
liberation of peoples they knew little and distrusted
much. They found their spokesman in Stalin and that
is probably why his popularity has not been diminished
by the elimination of Trotsky and his adherents. The
war has naturally fomented nationalism but aloofness
towards foreigners has always been a marked Russian
trait. This was particularly true of those who remained
after the liquidation of the ruling classes because the
latter alone had had contact with the West.

In the Eurasian continent Russia has always been
the meeting ground of East and West, both racially
and culturally, but, being never permanently subjugated by one or the other, has developed a nationalism that has considered itself to be *sui generis* (originally, probably, on the basis of Orthodoxy). This
nationalism, which drew all its material advances
from Europe, has always had an ambivalent attitude
towards the West. On the one hand the educated

classes sought 'culture' there and the bureaucracy was (at times) recruited thence, particularly from Germany, while on the other hand, Europeans were heretics and, to the peasant, enemies because they were foreigners. By ascribing the reactionism of the Tsarist system to foreign influence, nationalism and revolution could be the two sides of the coin of patriotism. As Sumner in his *Survey of Russian History* says: 'This contrast between Russia as a part of Europe and Russia as a world to herself with different values and different roots became all the more acute by the end of the nineteenth century when the educated minority was deeply divided within itself and the basis of civilized rule as earlier understood, i.e. European absolutism, was being more and more heavily attacked. Tsarism as a system of bureaucratic absolutist rule, with all its dark evils represented none the less Europe; for its enemies, the Europe of reaction or a Europe alien to the best part and the true genius of the Russian people.'

RUSSIAN SUSPICION OF FOREIGNERS

To this Europe and to the outer world generally the name of 'capitalism' has been given—inappropriately as we have seen. Since within Russia there is no longer any struggle between capital and labour—at least none that is labelled in these terms—and since the machinery of capitalism is actually used in Russian economy, we should expect the invidious sense of the term to lapse unless, as a symbol, it was a good camouflage for a deep-seated suspicion of foreigners. The more primitive a people are, the more do they regard strangers as suspicious characters. But the Russians have had a special reason for being hostile. For centuries the bulk of their land has been overrun time and again by invaders, now from the East and now from the West, who for varying periods subjugated all but the souls of the people. For them the word 'tyrants' is almost synonymous with 'foreigner'. Russians have never known peace as we have, and from the dawn of history rival marauders, conquerors and dynasties have struggled for brief ownership of one part or another of the territory that is now Russia, and none of them was long enough in possession to have established a political system that did not seem to the bulk of the people a device for their exploitation. Against such rulers there could be no open warfare, no struggle conducted under the rules of chivalry and no prospect of a peace with such a rearrangement of frontiers as to enable each belligerent to live peaceably in his own habitation. It was underground warfare, waged by secret police and arbitrary magistrates against sabotage and assassination. When one considers that this lasted for generations, long enough to become traditional, it is easy to understand certain aspects of Russian character. There is undying loyalty to one's mates but suspicion towards strangers who may be spies. Secondly the morals of war time are extended into the period of so-called peace. A promise is less an accepted obligation than a means of placating the enemy. A foreign diplomat is a spy and not a liaison officer; one's agents are engaged in trying to upset the enemy's economy, so presumably his are trying to do the same thing in return, and so on.

Before the last war the ramification of suspicion—theoretic or active—was so extensive and so matched by the permeation of the secret police into every social circle that strangers were inevitably people with whom one was reticent. The revolution not only increased this tendency to suspicion but made its projection on foreigners inevitable for two reasons. First, animosity towards the Tsarist regime was projected on a 'capitalistic' outer world, as we have seen, and secondly, Russia's late allies proceeded to justify this projection by support of the Whites. The probable importance of the latter can be deduced from the treatment of it by Strauss, a socialist who, perturbed by an alleged betrayal of Communism by the Russian bureaucracy, writes in his book *Soviet Russia* about the departure of the Bolshevists from the true faith of Communism. Although he accounts adequately for the difficulties facing the Communists in October 1918 and the years immediately following on the basis of war exhaustion and internal hostilities, he keeps harping on the persecution of the new Government by the hostile capitalistic powers who supported all the gangsters they could link up with in Russia. Although he does not say so explicitly, he seems to be implying that the Bolshevists might have been able to introduce real Communism had the Allies left them alone. His prejudice is further exhibited by his failure to mention the relief that was given by the same capitalists a few years later to the land that was devastated by famine and typhus. If a foreigner, merely because he is a socialist, has this bias, what should we not expect of those who had personally to fight the friends of the Whites as well as the Whites themselves?

There can be no doubt but that this distrust has been mutual. Our leaders have been working hard to remove it and with some success so far as most of the Allies are concerned, but with less result in Russia if a wealth of stories have any foundation in fact. There is no purpose served by our resenting this: we should recognise its inevitability, rooted as it is in Russian history, and adapt ourselves to the prospect of a long period during which every ostensibly friendly word or deed from the West will be interpreted as camouflage for insidious attacks on the sacred Communism of Russia. This is paranoid reasoning and there is no arguing with this kind of a lunatic, though we should remember that it is not one-sided. On the other hand, unjustifiable suspicion is peculiar to those who feel some inferiority, as the Germans do. Russia always has been inferior to Europe in material culture and therefore, and to that extent, has in the past had a psychological basis for suspicion. But, if that inferiority lapses, the background of distrust also goes and it becomes possible —in theory—for events to be evaluated objectively. Against this happy development, however, there is operating the terribly potent factor of ignorance.

SECRECY, CENSORSHIP AND
IGNORANCE

There has been censorship in Russia since the days of Peter the Great but it was not accompanied by positive propaganda till the Revolution. Before the first World War Russia was the only European country that could not be entered by a traveller without a passport. The origin of the isolation that kept foreigners ignorant of Russia and Russians ignorant of the outer world is easily understood. Government in Tsarist days was largely a matter of intrigue and therefore inevitably secretive. On the other hand the oppressed Left upheld doctrines regarded as treasonable, and so it had to work underground. So long as a movement cannot come into the open, it cannot organize sufficient material strength to challenge an efficient government. So it naturally turns to foreign aid or may be seduced into accepting help from an inimical foreign power. Thus the foreigner was to the Tsarist an actual or potential ally of the revolutionary and contact with him was reduced to a minimum. Once Communism was established the foreigner became a potential counter-revolutionary—and probably an actual one at times. The purge of generals which took place in June 1937 was not accompanied by public trial, and confessions were merely said to have been made. Whether the executed generals were Trotskyites or not we do not know nor does it now matter, because what moves people is not actual events but the interpretation people put on them. According to Ambassador Davies (*Mission to Moscow*) one rumour stated: 'There had been established a definite agreement between the Russian Generals and the German Reichswehr to cooperate with Germany as part of an impending "putsch" into the Ukraine; that this was part of a larger Trotsky plot for the purpose of destroying the Stalin regime through a foreign war so that a new buffer state between the Orient and Europe might arise therefrom to save "real" communism through the aid of the Red Army.' The purge did not quiet fears, for Davies wrote a year later (June 6th, 1938) of '...a condition bordering on panic. This government is obsessed by the idea that it is being isolated by a hostile world and that the hands of all capitalistic nations are against it....Thousands of foreign nationals have been arrested, imprisoned and held incommunicando'. This referred not only to Axis subjects, but also to English, French, Turks, Persians and Afghans. If there were in Russia sceptics as to the reality of plots between enemy agents and counter-revolutionaries—as there were plenty abroad —their arguments are now met by the apparent absence in Russia of fifth columnists to aid the invading Germans. The average Russians will probably believe to-day that Germans were plotting with anti-Stalinists in Russia and that the policy of distrusting foreigners was justified as events proved.

As a preparation for war, secrecy is invaluable and no country perhaps has ever achieved this 'security' as has Russia. It is reported that for years before

1941 a foreign military attaché tried to find out what the basic pay of the Russian soldier was but could never get an answer to this question about a fact known to countless millions. Cassidy (*Moscow Dateline*) says: 'All foreign experts were wrong about the Russian war potential because of proletariat reticence in dealing with the bourgeoisie.' On the other hand secretiveness makes an uneasy peace and, during a war, militates against cooperation with one's allies. Further the aloofness that inevitably accompanies reticence means an ignorance of what goes on abroad that may have serious results. Ignorance of matters in which one has interest is, psychologically, like the physical vacuum which nature abhors. The empty space is filled by fantasy or propaganda and the propagandist may even believe the stuff he makes up himself. One trivial and one serious example may illustrate the results of an aggressive isolationism. A couple of years before the war I chanced to listen to a Moscow broadcast in English addressed to the British working man. He was told that, thanks to the new regime, the Communist workman now had opportunities to play games; working men were brought to the microphone to explain to their British comrades what football, lawn tennis, etc., were like and urged them to strive for a system that would allow the working man familiarity with what, elsewhere in the world, were pastimes of the rich alone. Cassidy, who was in Russia when Hitler made his attack, avers that the Kremlin was definitely unprepared for the actual attack although repeatedly warned of it by the Allies; Sir Stafford Cripps tried to see both Stalin and Molotov to warn them of its imminence but was refused audience.

Against this aloofness and the ignorance it nourishes no ordinary propaganda can combat successfully, because prejudice always triumphs over argument, and statements as to alleged facts are always discounted when the source is suspect. Actual experience and the knowledge that becomes commonplace can alone dispel ignorance. Take our own case. In this country there was a widespread belief before the war that Russian industry was hopelessly inefficient. Russia always had been so, and Communism was too doctrinaire to have affected national competence. Further, except in the eyes of a minority, Communism was so revolutionary, so redolent of dictatorship and Godlessness as to be abhorrent. So there was incredulity for what publicity Moscow gave to its mechanization, and the tales of travellers who had visited Russia were discounted. What could a country accomplish that barred the import of foreign literature—even scientific publications? That incredulity is now gone, simply and solely because the Russians have been able to outmatch the Germans in military equipment. We realise that no matter what supplies we and the Americans might have been able to get to Russia, we could never have made good the deficiency that was inevitable in a country so industrially weak as the Russia we envisaged.

WILL IGNORANCE BE DISPELLED
OR FOSTERED?

Will the Russian people suffer any analogous change of opinion about their present Allies? It is unlikely that they can have personal experience extensive enough to weaken their prejudice. Not one in ten thousand of them will have had contact with an American or an Englishman. More, of course, will have become familiar with foreign equipment, but it is easy enough to dispose of that argument in favour of Anglo-Saxon assistance. Let us consider the situation dispassionately. Germany is beaten and then, wherever people indulge in idle chatter, the question is discussed as to who won the war. Unless human nature has changed radically the claims of one's own country will tend to rank higher than the claims of the alliance as a whole. The Russians will believe with justice that they suffered more than the British empire or America in blood, goods and territory. Even if this were untrue, it would be believed because the devastation one sees for onself is more real than what one merely hears about. Further they will think that they inflicted more injury on German arms than did the Anglo-Saxons: the truth will be something for historians to wrangle over for generations. So the Russians will believe that they won the war. For whom? For the U.S.S.R., of course. *They* were not fighting to keep the world safe for capitalism and democracy, so no more will they believe that their Allies were fighting for communism. If we gave Russia material aid the debt was more than repaid by the Russian blood spilled in defeating Germany, blood that otherwise would have flowed from Anglo-Saxon veins. Will any of our actions prove to the mass of the Soviet people that their belief in the hostility of all foreigners was ill-founded? It seems extremely unlikely. But, on the other hand, they will be sensitive to the policy followed by their own propaganda, as credulous of it as they will be incredulous of ours. So what line is the Kremlin likely to follow? Will it make as its directive 'We won the War' and claim that Anglo-Saxon aid had been more than repaid by the Russian destruction of German armies, thus providing the background for popular support of further armed conflict with the West; or will it publicize the Anglo-Saxon contributions to victory which would make popular the policy of cooperation—or at least of live-and-let-live—with capitalistic countries that, pre-war, were represented as enemies of Communism? One can approach an answer to this question only after considering more of the factors which go to make up the ethos of contemporary Russia. So we shall return to it later.*

Without an intimate knowledge of Stalin's character, such as no foreigner is likely to have, his purely personal contribution to the formation of policy cannot be predicted, but one may not unfruitfully speculate as to what the drift of Soviet

* See p. 81.

Weltanschauung would impose on a Stalin who travelled on and with the tide. There are two principles operating, principles that at some points may reinforce each other but sometimes conflict. The first is a realism that has been a striking feature of foreign policy since Stalin succeeded to power. Not only has the chimera of world-wide revolution been formally disavowed, but the basic Communist principle of everyone working only for the common good has been abandoned in most industries in favour of piece-rate wages that result in wide differences in the sharing of the necessities and amenities of life. The other factor is Russian religion—not its theology or its observances, but the way in which Russians have behaved in matters that fall, psychologically, into the religious category.

REALISM COUNSELS PEACE IN FUTURE

Realism should operate to make Russia avoid further war at almost any cost. The people have a beggarly standard of comfort while the territory that is indisputably Russian is, according to competent authorities, potentially richer than that of any other empire. She does not need to go overseas to get practically every raw material and, mechanization being now enthusiastically developed, she can go on exploiting her natural resources almost indefinitely. When one reads of the magnitude of Russian resources and the smallness of the population that owns them, the vision of economic possibilities becomes dazzling. Only one influence seems likely now to be a possible deterrent to the rapid development of these potentialities. That is war. If the U.S.S.R. were poorly furnished with natural resources, the preliminary economic expansion might be the seizure of Roumanian or Persian oil or conquest of the Dardanelles, so as to guarantee free passage for exports and imports. But Russia does not need extra oil so much as she wants opportunity to develop her heritage and she is so nearly self-supporting as to make foreign trade a similarly insignificant desideratum. The day is passed when she needed large quantities of foreign machinery and manufactures in order to maintain her economy. If the Russian were an 'economic man', that is if he were a pure realist, the gain of no major war would be counted as worth its cost.

THE CHARACTER OF RUSSIAN RELIGION

It is possible that religion is the most important factor in the history of Russia. Some authorities claim that there was no other nationalizing influence in the territory that became Muscovy and among the peoples inhabiting this region. No matter who the rulers might be, religion that was regarded as peculiarly Russian held the people together and knit them into a community. There are two aspects of Orthodoxy which are important in relation to our present problem. Christianity combines two elements that ideally are integrated together but actually tend to be divorced, so that one develops at the expense of the other. One is communion with the Divine mediated by sacraments, ritual worship, or (more rarely) mystical contemplation, while the other is ethical, stressing the responsibilities of the Christian to his fellows.

Orthodoxy has always been characterized by an emphasis on the supernatural benefits which the church can afford to the faithful rather than on the moral obligations which the faith entails. The passport to Heaven, or to its foretaste in worship, is faith, and, therefore, sanctity tends to be identified with purity and fervour of belief. Thus orthodoxy is all important. In pre-revolutionary days, heresy was accounted a greater sin than any infraction of human laws and this bias has been taken over by the U.S.S.R., which regards infidelity to the political faith as the most serious of crimes. The German, as represented in his caricature the Nazi, believes in a tribal God who favours Germans only. The Russian believes in a universal God, but one to whom there is only one correct and effective way of approach. So the Russians, too, are a chosen community, although not a chosen race ethnically. Heretics are enemies within the fold or foreigners who have not found the true Way. The devout Russian has had proof of the efficacy of his worship in his religious experience; he has also seen proof of divine favour in the downfall of powers that faltered in their faith. Muscovy was 'Holy Russia' because it had the one true faith and this was held to be proved when first Constantinople and then Greece fell. With the Schism (1667) Russian religious unity ended, but the 'orthodox' attitude lived on and became a factor in the political struggle which culminated in the 1917 revolution. The government and upper classes adhered to the official church which adopted new rituals, but the 'Old Believers', drawn chiefly from among the peasants and merchants, stood for the maintenance of the rituals of the 'true' Church of Holy Russia. Later, they ramified into many kinds of 'Non-Conformist' sects and often were allied with political disaffection. It was inevitable that the official church would have to go with the Revolution because it was inextricably bound with Tsarism.

But in Russian Communism (as separate and different from Marxism) there is no incompatibility between belief in the 'People' and belief in a God that, if not Russian, is at least worshipped in a peculiarly Russian way, which is the only right way, the way of 'Holy Russia', the way of the persecuted 'Old Believers'. Indeed the more the Russian Church is allowed to flourish the stronger is the national fervour likely to grow. Sumner (*Survey of Russian History*) says: 'Moscow became (early sixteenth century) not only ...the Third Rome, but "A Second Jerusalem", and the "Second Noah's Ark", the sole guardian and depository of true orthodoxy; and Russia became "Holy Russia" signifying the ideal of complete and unconditional loyalty to the faith accepted, a conception of orthodoxy somewhat akin to the orthodoxy of Communism.'

National Socialism and Christianity are incompatible because the former is built round the idea of a tribal god. But, as Davies says, 'the Christian religion could be imposed upon the communistic principles without its doing violence to its economic and political principles'. The original official antagonism to religion with its active propaganda in favour of godlessness had, probably, two determinations. The first was just one aspect of the general revolt against the previous established authority, much like the wholesale rebellion of an adolescent against everything his parents have stood for. When the adolescent has grown up and is governing his life according to a set of values that he has adopted as his own, he tends to be more tolerant of the ideals and principles of a generation that is no longer coercing him. It is no longer necessary for the Bolshevik regime to decry Christianity simply because the Tsarist government was Christian. No one would now accuse Stalin of being a traitor to the revolution if he grants an interview to the Patriarch. The second factor was probably less conscious but none the less potent for that. It was felt that Communism needed for its success so much of that kind of worship and devotion which is normally an expression of religious faith that allegiance could not be divided between God and the proletariat. Both Christianity and Communism strive for a brotherhood of man. If spiritual and economic brotherhood are held to be inseparable or if they are confused unthinkingly by fanatical socialists, then one can not serve both God and ' The People'. On the other hand if one is going to give unto Caesar only the things that are Caesar's, then it is quite possible for a Russian to maintain his faith and worship in a church whose kingdom is not of this world—a strong tendency in Orthodoxy—and at the same time to strive as a good Communist for the political unity and material betterment of the divers races that make up the U.S.S.R. So there are various possibilities in the directions which the evolution of Russian idealism may take.

ARE PUBLISHED CHANGES OF POLICY GENUINE?

It may be that both the formal abolition of the Comintern and the formal recognition of the Russian Church are bluffs, astute diplomatic moves to meet the exigencies of the war situation. This is what those say who are suspicious of everything the Kremlin does: toleration for the church increases the unity of patriotic service which is essential for maintaining the struggle against Hitler, while an ostensible abandonment of the Crusade to overthrow all 'capitalistic' governments throughout the world is a *quid pro quo* for Anglo-American assistance. In favour of this interpretation one can argue that it is consistent both with Kremlin morals and with the programme the Bolshevists undertook when obtaining power. As explained earlier, Communism was a war against existing institutions and as a war justified any kind of deceit that might promote victory. Expedience and not honour is the basis of the ethics of warfare. One can go further and argue that, even in times of peace, the good of any large and self-contained community is the ultimate standard of the people and that Russia always was a law unto itself morally. In support of the last argument it could also be urged that this was only natural in a country whose religion stressed the supernatural rather than the moral. So we should be uncritically charitable if we accepted these disavowals of earlier policy at their face value simply because the Kremlin could be trusted to keep its word. If the policies of the U.S.S.R. had shown no other changes we should have to regard the recognition of religion and the abandonment of world revolution as temporary political manœuvres. But so much else has changed and is changing.

NATIONAL TRENDS SURVIVE REVOLUTION

At any given moment in the history of a country its policies, although they may be promulgated as permanencies, belong to a process that is like the growth of a tree which is bound to develop according to the pattern of its species. Its stem may be cut and a graft implanted, but the graft will take only if it belongs to the same species, and the fruit which the scion bears is only a variety of that which is characteristic of the stock. Or the terminal bud of a conifer may be destroyed. For the moment it seems that the growth-habit of a tree has been changed and that it is going to spread sideways instead of maintaining its conical shape. But soon one of the side branches bends upwards to continue the central stem and, in after years, only a slight kink in the trunk gives evidence of what was, temporarily, a revolutionary change. Thus Russia seems now to be evolving a polity that is excluding what is foreign to its basic nature while it is adapting the new to the old so that a continuity of development becomes constantly more apparent. Nationalism is reasserting itself; as we shall see in a moment, isolationism is taking the place of an un-Russian kind of internationalism while Marxism is melting into a peculiarly Russian kind of Communism that is quite incompatible with the policies of the Third International. This compromise is, however, compatible with the recognition of the Church. Indeed Orthodoxy and nationalism can mutually support each other.

For this development there is precedent in the history of Slavism. This movement began with the Slavophiles two decades before the Crimean war. They believed in Orthodoxy and a non-European culture: their programme was a Messianic Russian salvation for the whole World. It was followed by pan-Slavism which began to show the influence of an isolationism proceeding from opposition to a government (under Alexander II) that flirted with Austria-Hungary. Emphasis shifted away from religion to politics animated by hostility to Germany and Hungary. Finally came neo-Slavism after the revolution of 1905. It dropped religion and was only potentially political, for it concentrated on the cultural unity of all Slavs with aims of economic cooperation. Its animus was largely anti-German. Thus an idealism that took the world for its parish evolved into a political and economic creed that was to unify a Slavic group and differentiate it from both West and East.

What would have happened to 'Slavism' had there been no first World War we cannot tell, but we do know that in the travail of that conflict Russia was brought to bed and was delivered of a child christened 'Communism', whose father was said to be Marx. But Marx is dead and Mother Russia is exercising her prerogative to bring up the posthumous child according to her interpretation of what Marxism means in actual practice. What are the elements which make up the character of this offspring and how are they, or can they be, portrayed in the propaganda handed out by the Kremlin to the Russian people? In other words what is the ideology on which the Bolshevists, no less than the Nazis, rely for the building up and maintenance of morale?

CHAPTER III

CONTEMPORARY OBJECTIVES AND METHODS IN RUSSIA

ECONOMIC EQUALITY?

In the forefront of the Russian system is communism in the sense of all property belonging to the community and not to the individual. This was the original ideal: labour produced all wealth, therefore all wealth should belong to the labourers. But the watchword, 'From each according to his ability, to each according to his needs' was found to be impracticable, and there is now individual ownership of many commodities and of money, while disparity in wages is actually encouraged. The formula should now read, 'From each according to his ability, to each according to his services'. Glaring inequalities in the scale of living result, but this is glossed over in two ways: all 'comrades', no matter whether they are privileged or live in penury, come from the 'People'; and all are serving the State. If one thinks that these are flimsy rationalizations, let one ponder on the facts that in this so-called capitalistic country, thanks to taxation both direct and indirect, it is only a small section of the populace which does not return the larger part of its earnings to the government and is therefore 'working for the people', while even in times of peace the bulk of all production is of commodities consumed by 'the people'. Yet we say that we work to make money for ourselves and our families and we value this 'right' highly. The words traditionally used to describe economic systems are of vastly greater importance psychologically than they are logically.

CENTRALIZED ECONOMIC CONTROL

'Ownership' is a slippery term, but it gains more than a propaganda value when it implies control over what is 'owned', be that either goods or labour. In Russia Communism means state control of economy and on broad lines this is an accomplished fact—a working system. Although there are many exceptions there seems to be no doubt but that the major industries in Russia are initiated, supported or suppressed by Moscow. The criterion for maintenance or abolition is not immediate gain as measured in money but the present or future good of the state. This is similar to the judgment of the 'City' in our system of ultimate economic value, but the Commissars have the advantage of being able to keep 'uneconomic' ventures going by pumping money into them derived from paying industries for an indefinite period, and they can control labour by forced migration or starvation with a ruthlessness ascribed to capitalists but beyond their power to achieve. In this country there has been a good deal of an analogous interference with the immediate operation of the law of supply and demand through subsidies, discriminative taxation, import duties, etc. But this is clumsy as compared with the Russian direct action. We are prone to be suspicious

of state control because we do not trust its efficiency
—which may be, psychologically, a rationalization—
but fundamentally because it is incompatible with
personal liberty, a belief in which is essential for our
morale. The Russians, however, never having known
individual liberty, bow to the *force majeure* of the State,
are comforted by the freedom the proletariat has won,
and glory in the triumphs of state control. (Whether
this complacency can endure is another story.) So far the
individual economic liberty, which it has been found
expedient to grant, finds no place in Communist ideology. The myth is maintained that all work for the State,
just as we maintain the myth that we are free agents.

THE RECRUITMENT OF LEADERS

Another important element in the U.S.S.R. system is
its organization which in all fields adopts the hier-
archical distribution of authority and responsibility
which we are used to in military service. The Nazis,
having adopted a similar regimentation of all individuals, have dowered it with supernatural po-
tentiality and christened it the 'Führerprinzip'. The
power of all loyal followers is incorporated in the
leader who thus becomes the superman, while the
leader, thus inflated, is dowered with the wisdom
which inspires his orders. The magic works at all
levels, but, of course, reaches a practically divine level
at the apex of the pyramid where stands *the* Führer.
(The factual basis of this theory is represented in
the old claim of sociologists that a well-integrated

group develops something more than the algebraic sum of the individual contributions of all its members, something that belongs to the group as such and coerces a unanimity of group behaviour.) Although —so far as I know—the Russians have invented no such term as Führerprinzip, they have nevertheless made the production of leaders an essential part of their programme. As in Germany, a search is made in the primary schools for those who seem to have within them the potentialities of leadership, and these promising lads are then given special training and discipline analogous to that offered in our public school education. Those who justify the tuition are taken into the Party, given more and more responsibility, and may eventually become members of the Central Executive. With authority goes privilege. Actually the Soviets are governed by an aristocracy, although not an hereditary one, but that word is of course anathema. Even Stalin is still a 'comrade', which is excellent propaganda—for propaganda fights with and against words.

In the Tsarist days a serf had to have incredible luck and consummate ability to become a member of the ruling classes. Now all leaders can come from a citizenry that has been purged of its 'ruling classes'. Therefore the proletariat rules. Inevitably ideas about aristocracy and plutocracy are derived from the Tsarist regime: obviously countries that are admittedly capitalistic and still have 'classes' exclude from government all members of the proletariat, and censorship sees to it that the ordinary Russian is never disillusioned on this point. But his ignorance of the fact that a foreign workman may become a Cabinet Minister does not mean that he is unjustified in believing that the net which gathers in potential leaders is cast wider over the (surviving) population than in the countries where there is a *de facto* or a legally recognised class system. So long as the Communist aristocrat is regarded as one of the people, his position is secure and with the power he has in his hands he can do much to entrench this system. Under any kind of government the masses will always be ruled, benevolently or selfishly, and in a sense exploited, by those in authority. If every one with initiative is taken into the ruling class, potential rebel leaders are bribed into conservatism. The bribe in a bureaucracy is vastly greater than in any pluto-cracy or democracy where laws can restrict the power of the financier and votes can overthrow the politician. Where legislation and executive authority are in the same hands, the opportunities for the ambitious man far exceed those which any industrialist or statesman can look forward to in a democracy. Paradoxically it is "Communism" which offers the greatest scope to individualism.

WHERE NATIONAL SOCIALISM AND COMMUNISM PART COMPANY

Because both Germans and Russians have a similar organization they are often presumed to have a similar outlook *vis-à-vis* the rest of the world.

Actually, however, their aims are disparate because the Nazis link the Führerprinzip with the Herrenvolk myth while the Bolshevists link it with the Proletarian myth. The latter is based on a curious argument: all wealth is the product of labour (which with appropriate definition can be accepted as true); so labour has a 'right' to all wealth (here a problem in ethics is introduced that is not so easily reduced to syllogisms); if labour everywhere were given this right, mankind would be redeemed (which is just as much a truth as 'economic man' is a reality). The practical conclusion is that liquidation of capitalists and enthronement of the proletariat will put the world to rights. (The facts that labour producing wealth includes management and is not the same as the labour of the proletariat escape the notice of the enthusiast.) The scientific and logical criticisms of these beliefs, although they have been published in millions of words, have no bearing on what might be called their pragmatic validity. The Herrenvolk myth involves the German inevitably in war. The Proletarian myth may lead to revolution and therefore to war, but it is essentially a missionary programme, a scheme for the betterment of mankind.

INFLUENCE OF IDEOLOGY ON SCIENTIFIC WORK

An excellent example of this difference is its reaction on biological theory. If there is a superior race, then its virtue is hereditary and mankind can be improved by selective breeding. In Germany this view has not only rationalized the persecution of the Jews and the enslavement of 'non-Aryans' but has inspired special marriage laws and an intensive study of genetics. On the other hand in the making of the individual there are operating environmental factors which affect growth, health and competence; and to weigh the relative importance of heredity and environment is a task as important for the dispassionate biologist as it is for the stock-raiser, the educationist, the doctor, or the practical reformer. Dispassionateness, however, is incompatible with demagoguery: one cannot have a political faith expressed in slogans about the interaction of two variables. The theories which move the masses have to be all white or all black. No theory that justifies the elevation of the proletariat can include the notion that people may be born inferior. Consequently Russian Communism stresses the importance of environment to the exclusion of heredity; it says that all races and all families are equal. Education and opportunity are all that is necessary to elevate the apparently inferior folk. Naturally, therefore, the controlled science of the U.S.S.R. has striven to rationalize this one-sided view, as is illustrated in two examples.

Among the few Tsarist scientists allowed to survive in Russia was Pavlov, the physiologist known to the lay world as the discoverer of the 'conditioned reflex' and, therefore, as the instigator of 'behaviourism' in psychology. Strictly speaking a reflex is a bodily response, depending on nervous mechanisms that are part of the inherited nervous system equipment. What is called a 'conditioned reflex' is an analogous reaction produced psychologically and implanted by training. The phenomenon was first reported by an English physiologist, Sherrington, but not given any name by him. Pavlov rediscovered the phenomenon and labelled it a 'conditioned reflex'. In vain do physiologists point out that the phenomenon is not a reflex; the term has caught on and persists in spite of its implications. When one considers its relevance to Communist theory, it seems that, in Russia, the term has been popularized because of its implications. If it be a reflex, it is mediated presumably by definite pathways in the brain. If these can be made by training, then education has accomplished a change in brain structure of a kind previously assumed to be wholly inborn. Thus Pavlov's work gave 'scientific' support to the Communist ideology that favoured education at the expense of heredity. So Pavlov's life was not only spared but, at the time when the U.S.S.R. was most impoverished, he had extensive laboratories built for him and was given unlimited facilities for his work. (The work was undoubtedly important, but its physiological conclusions have been shown to be untenable, and it has been claimed that they were based on selected experimental results.)

With this may be compared the fate of work undertaken at the Maxim Gorki Medical Psychological Institute in Moscow. There is only one field in which the relative importance of inheritance and environ-

ment in human development can be clearly discriminated and that is in a study of so-called one egg
twins who have been reared in separate and dissimilar
environments. Some years ago a large scale attack
on this problem was begun in the Maxim Gorki
Institute and some interesting results were published.
Then about six years ago this research was suddenly
abandoned. 'According to the most reliable information available, the director of the Institute and
some of his associates got into trouble with the
governmental authorities and disappeared. No one
seems to know what became of them. It was rumoured
that the ruling authorities regarded the results of the
published research as too favourable to heredity and
not sufficiently favourable to environment. They
thought that the work so far done savoured too much
of the unpopular race-biology of the Germans.'* In
contrast to this it is interesting to note that the only
extensive studies that have ever been made of
criminality in twins have been in Germany and, what
is more, in Nazi Germany.

We may call this a prostitution of science or we
may regard science as maid of all work who naturally
must carry out orders, but we cannot afford to be
indifferent to the influence such ideologies have on
international relationships. If heredity is all important, there can be no doubt but that mankind
would be best served if government were everywhere
in the hands of a superior race, selectively bred to
preserve and increase its capacity for rule while those

* H. H. Newman, *Twins and Supertwins.*

who are governed were bred so as to fit them for the performance of their menial tasks. On the other hand, if education and opportunity can elevate the masses, then mankind would be best served if the system which would guarantee them were everywhere installed. This, however, implies no overlordship for the promulgators of the system; they are missionaries not conquerors, and their religion is a catholicism because it takes in all colours and all races. The black, the brown, the yellow, the red and the white Communists are all equal—once they are Communists. The more extensive the field the more inspiring is the ideal which its exploitation represents. Both Germans and Russians have been exalted by a vision of an extension of their systems to cover the whole world. But if they are both forced to limit the range of their operations the effects on them will be quite different on account of their geographic and racial situations. Germany is a small country with a relatively homogenous population. Confined within their borders the Herrenvolk can, if they like, kill off all non-Aryans and live in their little Olympus. But then the superman claim becomes as ludicrously unreal as an army composed only of generals. On the other hand Russia is so vast as to be a world of itself. Communism could work for generations in the perfection of its system at home and still leave incomplete its tasks of welding together its diverse peoples in the service of a single political ideal, of educating its millions of illiterates up to a secondary school standard, and of exploiting to the full its matchless natural resources. Russia does not need to fear peace as an end to its ideology. The Third International can die without Communism abandoning its essential and idealistic aspirations.

THE ACCEPTABILITY OF A NATIONAL 'SOCIALISM'

A revolution which not only changes the personnel of government but also inaugurates a new polity seems to release great energies. The people have something new to live for, the revolutionary ideal is inspiring. It might therefore be expected that were this ideal abandoned, enthusiasm would lapse. But this seems unlikely to happen now in the U.S.S.R. for several reasons. One is that the change from a universal to a national goal has been gradual and has been rationalized as the temporary expedient of first proving the practicability of Communism at home before foisting it on the world. Further it has been forced on Russia by the German attack—only a fervent nationalism could have saved the country from extinction. People's memories are short and there has been no rival party to point out the inconsistency between the original International Communism and a national socialism. Moreover the average Russian has little reason to be interested in foreigners and much to be interested in the welfare of his own parish and the country with which it has become linked. The effect of the revolution has been to make him aware of the mutual dependence of his parish and the vast land of which it is a part, while isolationism is more natural to the Russian than is internationalism. Finally the new type of policy works. Not only has it been associated with the greatest military achievements in Russian history, it also is offering a promise of a higher standard of comfort, one that the serf or factory worker had regarded as chimerical. The potentialities of mechanization are everywhere apparent, and in ignorance of living standards elsewhere it must seem to the untravelled labourer that his lot will shortly be better than that of the wage slave in any capitalistic country. Natural resources are vast enough to cover an enormous rise in the standard of comfort even if they are tapped inefficiently. If the proof of the pudding is in the eating there is every reason to expect that the quondam serf will find national Communism a good pudding.

A NEW COMMUNIST 'ORTHODOXY'

The turning point in the history of revolutionary Russia came with Stalin and the Five-Year Plans. The country was bankrupt and could not afford to subsidize international revolt on a scale large enough to be effective. If Russia was to survive it had to exploit its potential wealth, and this could not be done without the assistance of experts and their equipment from capitalistic countries. It was not feasible to dishonour debts, threaten the creditor, and expect him to offer further aid. Whatever happened to world Communism its Russian exponents had tacitly, at least, to abandon that programme. The Gordian knot was cut when Stalin excommunicated Trotsky. If this term is justifiable it has an important implication for future policy. It stamps International Communism as being schismatic and, perhaps, even heretical. What will this mean for the Communists abroad? They must either migrate to Russia and be naturalized there or else belong to a schismatic sect. When, as seems quite possible, the wealth of that great empire is more fully exploited, will the members of this rich communion want to share their wealth with heretics: that is, will they spend money to further the agitation of self-styled 'Communists' abroad? (A possible answer might be to point to the Soviet intervention in Spain, but that, in view of the military resources of Russia that were later revealed, was a half-hearted assistance and may well have been actuated by the ambitions of embarrassing Germany and gaining some first-hand knowledge of technical military developments.)

In this connection a pertinent analogy is to be found in the traditional behaviour of the Orthodox Church. It has had no doubt as to its being the one true form of Christianity, but has not been aggressive in its rivalry with other confessions. Missionaries have, through the centuries, accompanied the explorers, traders and settlers who extended Russian dominion eastwards, but efforts to convert schismatics and heretics outside Russia have been at best fitful and short-lived. When one remembers that East and West were once one church, this is in remarkable contrast to the behaviour of Rome, which is equally interested in the conversion of the pagans and reclaiming the souls of heretics anywhere. This contrast is not based on specific theological differences which divide Roman Catholicism from Russian Orthodoxy, but has been ascribed rather to the political habits of the Holy Roman Empire and of Russia.

ISOLATIONISM

Some fifty-five years ago Leroy-Beaulieu wrote: 'Isolation is becoming to Russian greatness.... Russia is bent on finding everything within herself; she considers herself a world apart, or rather as the centre of gravity of the coming world' (*The Empire of the Tsars and the Russians*, Part III). Isolationism is perhaps the keynote of the U.S.S.R. symphony. In this connection it is important to keep in mind two facts: that there are operating in Russia to-day many traditions built up during centuries and that the traditions that survive, or are reasserting themselves after the revolution, are those buried deep in the nature of the existing population, i.e. in the survivors after migration and liquidation have removed the upper classes and the bulk of the bourgeoisie. In other words they are the peasants and children of the peasantry that did not like being pushed about by landlords who spoke French or some other foreign tongue to mark their superiority and 'culture'. They resented regimentation at the hands of officials many of whom were foreigners (particularly Germans). In so far as they knew the origin of bureaucratic methods, they would realize that their rulers were inspired by foreign influence and that court circles were forever flirting with foreign powers. They wanted to be left alone to practise their husbandry and to have peace. Not only did foreign contacts seem always to result in war; even the tyranny from which they suffered in times of peace seemed to be associated with foreigners or foreign influence.

Among the survivors of the revolution were left-wing intellectuals who must still have some share in forming public opinion. The intellectuals had, of course, much more contact with the outer world and sought it. Yet there was enough ambivalence in their attitude towards Westernism to make isolationism a possibility for them too. They felt, as Russians, an inferiority of their people in the niceties and arti-ficialities of civilization but, on the other hand, had pride in the immensity of their country and confidence in its intellectual virility. The bias of this class leaned towards Slavism in one of its forms and, as we have seen, this movement eventually developed belief in a culture that was purely Slavic, superior because it was Slavic, but intended for Slavs alone.

In addition to these specifically Russian factors in favour of isolationism there are general ones that operate in any very large continental area that is under one government. Both knowledge of the world and moral standards are acquired in two ways. First there is education in the formal sense, which is given by instruction, precepts and discipline in the home and school which may be supplemented, so far as the acquisition of information is concerned, by one's private reading. Second there is direct experience, whereby a man learns for himself; with this is coupled the gradual and involuntary imitation of one's fellows in the ethical field which leads to the notorious phenomenon of different communities having quite different moral codes. The results of formal education are apt to remain objective and impersonal with relatively little influence on opinion and behaviour, while personally gained knowledge has a potent feeling of reality attached to it and the morals which one absorbs unwittingly form the basis, if not the totality, of 'conscience'. It follows that, functionally, one's intellectual and moral outlook corresponds to that of the group with which one is in contact. It makes up the world that matters for any individual. In a small country whose economy involves constant contact with foreigners, the 'world' is not composed simply of one's compatriots. Events take place in distant lands that do matter, and there are admitted to be peoples abroad whose ambitions and antipathies have to be reckoned with. On the other hand in huge areas like America, China or Russia, the average citizen may pass his life without ever seeing or speaking to a foreigner and, except in the case of a major war, may never feel the impact of any foreign event. Education can, of course, teach a man that there are other countries, although if education is tendentious and linked with censorship the knowledge may be false, but at best, and without personal experience, the foreign land tends to be distant and unreal as is another inhabited planet in the solar system. This simile, of course, expresses the tendency in an exaggerated form; but for millions of Russians it may actually approximate the truth. We should remember that illiteracy is still common in Russia and that its amelioration has been accompanied by a censorship that excludes, or doctors, information from abroad. To the average 'comrade' Russian views on matters political, scientific or moral must constitute the truths that are basic to 'civilization'. If there are foreigners who know not these truths they must be uneducated or wilfully blind.

NATIONALISM PROMOTES ISOLATIONISM

All these considerations bear on the genuineness— or falsity according to persistent German propaganda —of the Kremlin's abandonment of the Comintern. Be it only as a result of the war, nationalism must have gained at the expense of internationalism. If, further, both tradition and geographic situation tend to produce isolationism it will be difficult for Stalin or his successors to reverse the trend. Moreover there is the *post hoc ergo propter hoc* argument which sways people emotionally even against their critical judg-ment. The greatest misery that the Russians had ever known was in the years immediately after the revolution. This was the period when world-wide dominance of the proletariat was the published ideal of the U.S.S.R. That a return to internationalism would mean a return to the horrors of that period is an argument that is likely to operate even though it might never be explicitly formulated. Its disguise would be: Why toil and slave for the benefit of foreigners?—charity begins at home. Thus the common man. A similar attitude is likely in the intellectual who must have his formulae and the rationalizations to maintain them. So long as Russia was regarded as a backward and therefore negligible country, the Trotskyist Communist must have felt that moral backing for his ideology would come from the spread of Communist doctrines abroad. He did not believe in Russia, only in a theoretic Communism. But now both Russia and Communism are vindicated so that conversion of the capitalistic countries ceases to be a psychological necessity. The intellectual can now find his rationalization for Communism in isolationism: let the poor benighted capitalists stew in their own juice till they come to their senses.

HOME PROPAGANDA WILL REFLECT FOREIGN POLICY

We may now revert for a moment to a question that we left earlier in mid-air, namely how the Kremlin would answer the question, Who won the war?* It will be recalled that there was every reason to suppose that, left to themselves, the Russian people would believe they had won the war and owed little to American and British aid, so that no feelings of gratitude

* See p. 54.

would inhibit such hostility towards us as might flare up again in some post-war situation. Against this danger there was little we could do to educate the Russian living behind closed frontiers and insulated by censorship from foreign influence. These very conditions, however, imply a compensatory sensitivity to domestic propaganda. If the Kremlin has decided on a live-and-let-live isolationism, indifference rather than hostility must be made to characterize the attitude of Russians towards foreigners. With much in the past to have created hostility (including much Bolshevik propaganda) that animosity will have to be neutralized by teaching the Russian that the Allies are not malevolent fiends. This will be particularly important if peace-terms or other post-war adjustments involve a compromise of Russian interests. So the genuineness or spuriousness of Russia's swing from internationalism to nationalism may be revealed soon in what prominence the Kremlin gives in its news to Allied victories and to Allied aid to Russia.

CHAPTER IV

THE FUTURE OF COMMUNIST RUSSIA: FOREIGN POLICY

So far a number of factors have been considered which have operated to produce the U.S.S.R. as it is to-day. Were this analysis complete and accurate the present status of the country would be thoroughly understood and its behaviour in the future could be predicted with confidence. That is because, as has been explained, we are dealing with a process that becomes visible in a series of events. The influences which caused any event in the past, did not cease to operate when the event was accomplished: they co-operated with the effects of that event to produce its successors, the resemblances and differences of the events constituting the evidence from which the factors have been deduced. When a mathematician has accounted fully for the forces that had moved a body to a series of positions, he can construct a curve which represents its pathway, and, if his equation is the right one, it not only accounts for any given observed position, but also makes possible prediction of future positions with equal accuracy. In non-mathematical sciences such accuracy is not possible because of the difficulty of discerning all the factors and the impossibility of evaluating them in quantitative terms. But that does not invalidate the general principle which one might state as: in so far as one can explain the occurrence of events in a connected series to the same extent can one predict later events in the series. Prediction is implicit in explanation. So this essay would be incomplete without some guesses as to what Russia is going to be like internally and what rôle she is likely to play in the post-war world.

Historical parallels are apt to be misleading because no other country has ever been placed in the same situation. The closest analogy is, perhaps, to the United States when it began to build a self-contained empire by migration into unexploited territory. But the early settlers in the eastern states had an entirely different Weltanschauung. They sought to build a state that would give the greatest possible freedom to the individual; they did not strive to serve a paramount state. Japan also provides a dubious parallel. In both Muscovy and Nippon there has been introduced a leaven of Western industrialization. But Japan is a tiny country, easily overpopulated, whereas Russia has a smaller population compared to its exploitable area than any other part of the world. Moreover, Russia is not obsessed by any Herrenvolk myth. Russia is sufficiently unique to justify prediction on the basis of her intrinsic peculiarities rather than by using comparisons with incompletely similar countries. What are these peculiarities?

PECULIARITIES OF RUSSIA

The uniqueness of the present Russian situation is based on a *combination* of the following conditions.

(1) There is an isolationism natural to a large continental country accentuated by historical influences and fortified by censorship. It may be assumed that the welfare of the U.S.S.R. will determine the moral judgement of its inhabitants. (2) There is a state control of an enormous economy as a permanent and not merely war-time measure. (3) Government is in the hands of a non-hereditary aristocracy, that is, it is a bureaucracy whose members are chosen without reference to birth and trained specifically for a leadership that is associated with the usual privileges of leaders. (4) These rulers are unfettered by any obligations entered into by previous governments. (5) There is an avowed basic policy of proving that national Communism will work, but there is a commitment to no other internal or external policy. (6) The government has an actual freedom of action and an unprecedented opportunity for prosecution of its internal policies because the country is so nearly self-sufficient economically and has enormous military power. When the war ends, it is safe to assume, there will be no surviving predatory power, the remaining great powers being pacific in tendency even were they to be suspicious or unfriendly. (7) There is not merely a popular acceptance of the government but an active support for it based on real enthusiasm as well as knowledge (without resentment) of the fact that non-cooperation means liquidation. (8) The potential wealth of the country is so prodigious that it could cover a good deal of inefficiency in production or stupidity in its planning.

Bankruptcy is highly improbable. (9) The peoples of the U.S.S.R. are not bound together by a common language, race, colour or creed but by such force as the government can exercise and by such common ideology as can be disseminated. Particularly in the Asiatic portion of the country, there are probably large sections of the population to whom such terms as 'capitalism' and 'proletariat' have no meaning. But the Communist propagandists have likely been able to make these words refer to local discontents and envies. Local minorities, for instance religious ones, are not necessarily protected from persecution by the representatives of the central government.

In a word it can be said that never in the history of political experiment has so much power been placed in the hands of so few men. But the power is not limitless. Inevitably tradition controls the bureaucrats unconsciously, while it must tend to slow down the operation of radical innovations when it does not make them actually impossible. The degree in which non-cooperation has forced basic modifications in socialist policy is already a matter of history. In this connection, too, one must bear in mind that a revolutionary government is always unstable; for lack of experience it has to proceed by trial and error, and radical changes appear in an accelerated evolution until the period that is dominated by experiment has passed and stability is reached. Thus some of the features of the present U.S.S.R. listed above are probably impermanent and others may become mani-

fest in the future. One of these has not been mentioned as yet because its existence—so far as my information goes—is a matter of hearsay. Some recent
visitors to Russia claim that a military caste has
grown up with an attitude of Prussian-like superiority
to civilians; that while the National Socialists in
Germany have been increasing the political control
of the Wehrmacht, the reverse process has been
taking place in Russia. In so far as this is true, or in
so far as it may be so, it would have great import for
the future.

REALISM IN POLICY

Having abandoned the cause of the World's Proletariat, the Kremlin will concentrate on the strengthen-
ing of national Communism, i.e. the well-being of its
own people particularly in the economic sphere will
be its first concern. For the first time in history we
see a government serving not an ambitious dynasty,
nor a religion, nor preserving a traditional way of
life, but aiming at a goal that is primarily economic.
Now, in contrast to all other aims, economic ones are
pursued in a realistic manner. Motives are less mixed
than when loyalty to 'honour' or to a religion or
considerations of reputation and prestige complicate
policy. Russia, for reasons already discussed, can
afford to neglect foreign opinion. Unlike Germany,
which is forever publishing tedious excuses for its
actions, the U.S.S.R. has now more than ever no
basis for any feeling of inferiority and justifies its

behaviour solely on the basis of internal expedience. It is a law to itself. So *realism* can dominate Russian planning as it has never done before in world history. The nearest parallel to the Kremlin is the board of directors of some huge corporation whose avowed objective is money-making. Every project will be subjected in the first instance to the criterion, Will it pay? This does not mean that every factory, or every department of every factory, in a huge combine must pay: some may be deliberately run at a loss but in the interest of the total industry—for instance research laboratories. Realism, not sentiment, such as prestige or pity for the oppressed minority, comes into consideration.

SENTIMENT IN POLICY

But no sooner has this generalization been made than it must be qualified. The naturally dishonest manufacturer may deteriorate his product when he thinks he can get away with it, or he may pay a bill only when he intends to deal with that creditor again, but actually when any concern has been going for some time its members tend to develop an esprit de corps that takes pride in the quality of the products and the reliability of its undertakings. Thus, although in the Lenin period the U.S.S.R. had no hesitancy in contracting debts it made no attempt to pay, when Stalin had nationalized the country Russia became a customer who paid debts promptly and without exception. This was, of course, a good and necessary policy but its result is likely to be a tradition of honesty in external commercial transactions at least. That its 'honour' will carry it much further seems doubtful. The Kremlin will argue as part of its realism that treaty obligations have never been honoured by any country except when self-interest was bound up with meeting the obligation—for cynicism always characterizes the 'realist' and, like Hitler, the dictator of the moment will argue that the only honour binding on a government is loyalty to the interests of the State. One may feel confident that such a conception of honour would be held in any thoroughly isolationist country.

RESTRICTION OF TERRITORIAL AMBITIONS

So, if we assume a basic tendency for economic expedience to govern policy, it would be profitable to foresee where sentiment would cut across this. Expedience would justify the annexation of territory that would contribute as least as much to the wealth of the U.S.S.R. as the seizing of it would cost, and included in the costs would be an estimate of the liability represented by the hostility of other great powers and the nuisance of having to digest hostile populations. Further, reasonable precautions against attacks by hostile powers would demand an extension of the border far enough from Leningrad to give that important industrial centre immunity against a sudden attack. One wants room in which to build fortifications.

But, with the exception of Leningrad's defence zone, it is unlikely that the business man's judgment would countenance any material advance beyond the pre-1939 frontiers. Tsarist Russia, being a non-industrialized country, was dependent on foreign trade for essential needs and so always had its eyes on guaranteeably free shipping routes—the Baltic and the Dardanelles. But now a minute fraction of surplus Russian production would, if exported, cover all necessary imports. She will be unique in the world in her economic self-sufficiency, not merely for the moment, but for generations to come. Her imperialistic expansion naturally takes the form of exploiting the huge natural resources that lie untouched within her present borders. She can shut her gates and, instead of being starved out, become richer. Should prestige and ambition urge occupation of the Dardanelles, the objection might well be raised in Kremlin conferences that the Dardanelles alone would give no reliable access to the outer world. One would need the Aegean islands and, if they were seized, they in turn would require Greece and Asia Minor for their protection, and so it would go on until possession of Gibraltar became a necessity. In other words the realist would argue that control of the Dardanelles was the very sign and symbol of imperialism, and isolationism is incompatible with imperialism. (This is well illustrated in the United States where strong isolationist sentiment has fought against the taking over of any territory beyond American shores, has wanted to get rid of the Philippines, and has studiously avoided interference with Mexico—in spite of many provocations—because no one knows where that would end.) The only territory worth acquiring is that which is rich in resources or contains a population of useful workers, sufficiently friendly or tractable to be readily adapted to the U.S.S.R. economy. Viewed from this angle the Roumanian oil fields would offer the only tempting prize. If Russia had little oil, or if it were available only thousands of miles to the east, or if the Ukraine were without its water power and coal, the Kremlin would doubtless consider Roumania essential to Russian prosperity. And what would it cost? Oil installations are vulnerable to air attack and one does not want to have them within a few minutes' flight of foreign aerodromes. So, if the Soviet politicians look ahead they would think of the problem of defence for these fields, a defence that could be secure only if the Russian borders were extended far beyond Roumania itself. In other words, this is an asset, like guaranteeable access to overseas highways, that could be secured only after an indefinite territorial expansion. The same argument would make it appear improbable that the Kremlin would complicate its external relations by trying to seize the oilfields of Persia, Irak and Arabia. Russia is big enough and rich enough as it is.

PRESTIGE CLAIMS

But this is to argue as if Russia had by its revolution achieved an unemotional rationality as perfect as

Sir Norman Angell's. As has been mentioned even hard-headed business men are prone to be affected by sentiment, so we can hardly expect the crusaders of a new economy to be immune to it. Thus the question to be answered is: What kind of sentiment is likely to cut across economic expediency? A truly isolationist country is not going to be bothered much with moral obligations to foreign states because the one moral criterion it recognizes is the welfare of its own people. Similarly, the maintenance of prestige is not likely to worry unduly a people that feels itself superior to the rest of the world in material wealth, fighting capacity, and sanity of political outlook. There remains loyalty to the ideals that are felt to be both the *raison d'être* and the inspiration of the national organization. If the pursuit of these ideals led to conflicts with other peoples, pride would be likely to triumph over caution. So long, therefore, as the Comintern was influential, Russia was likely to be embroiled in war. But with the advent of Stalin's national socialism that danger waned, although it has not disappeared because the area in which this economic gospel has to be practised is still undefined.

The original field for the immediate application of Communism was the Tsarist empire or such part of it as the revolutionary armies could gain or control. So far as the West was concerned this meant the old empire less Finland, the Baltic States and Poland. For twenty-two years, while Communism was being developed with enthusiasm and more or less success in the Versailles-bounded Russia, a feeling of proud independence of, and hostility to, the U.S.S.R. and of cultural and economic superiority to it was growing ever stronger in these previously Russian lands. If they were all now swallowed at one gulp the mass might prove to be indigestible even in Russia's capacious paunch. And why bother? The Kremlin is not interested in maintaining the prestige of the Tsarist empire. It is, however, morally bound to support its co-religionists in these lands. Before 1939, these were a handful of malcontents, but in that year, as in 1940, the situation changed. Russia occupied considerable areas in these states and set up Communist regimes. The people were forced to do at least lip service to the new system and some of course collaborated wholeheartedly either out of conviction or, becoming local officials, out of self-interest. Under any other aegis than that of Moscow these converts are, or will be, persecuted. So it becomes the duty of Russia to rescue them. This sentiment will, I suspect, triumph over all consideration of expedience because it will be sincere. The outer world may be shocked and regard the 'rescue' as being a flimsy pretext for sheer acquisitiveness. But the critics will have uneasy consciences if they recall the period—not so long distant—when indemnities were demanded for the murder of Christian missionaries.

If we wish to understand the Russian point of view in such an affair we should translate 'Communist' into 'Christian' and remember the reaction of many Englishmen to the persecution of the Armenians by the Turks. Were there not many who regarded it as a duty that Britain as a Christian power should make war on Turkey, punish the infidel and rescue the Christian? The children of these would-be crusaders will say that that was disinterested while the Russian seizure of these disputed regions would be predatory and the 'rescue' an excuse. But, if this argument is used, it will fall on deaf ears in Russia where religion and political aggrandizement have always been mutually self-supporting. In the days of the Tsars although all religions had statutory liberty, other laws and traditional practice curtailed that liberty. The Orthodox Church could make converts but other sects or religions were forbidden by law to do so. It was illegal to leave the Orthodox Church but not to disavow any other faith. Where, as in Poland or the Baltic States, there was much Roman Catholicism or Lutheranism, converts to Orthodoxy received political favours such as relative relief from taxation. Political and ecclesiastical interests were intertwined, each was an instrument for the aggrandizement of the other. All peoples, and particularly those who have little contact with the outer world, project their moral principles on all mankind as universally recognized truths, as 'human nature'. When the foreigner disputes these principles he is sacrilegious or insincere in alleging the existence of another code which would justify his actions. So the Russian will believe that everywhere the furtherance of ideals is used as an excuse for obtaining material advantage and that only the hypocrite disputes this. To some extent the Russian may be right, but it is important for us to bear in mind that this kind of what we call dishonesty or intellectual dishonesty is a permanent Russian trait. As Leroy-Beaulieu commented more than fifty years ago: 'With the wildest dreams of religious illuminism or political Utopias, the Russian frequently combines most practical calculations.'

INTERNATIONAL COMMITMENTS

Since National Communism was substituted for the international variety Russia has been a customer who paid her debts. There is no doubt that honesty is the best policy in business, provided one is going to continue doing business. But, if Russia is going isolationist, will she honour agreements now made with her Allies or is she making them merely to facilitate the lease-lend advantages now enjoyed with no intention of honouring them when they would stand in the way of her ambitions? It would take a far-sighted prophet to answer these questions with confidence, but there is evidence to suggest that she intends to follow the letter at least of such commitments as she will enter into. Apparently the Kremlin is cautious about making promises as the intentional swindler is not, yet it has given undertakings that— as we are likely to interpret them—would seem to be at variance with annexation of territory in the Polish and Baltic regions. Article V of the Soviet-British Treaty of May 26, 1942 established the principles of 'Not seeking territorial aggrandizement for themselves and of non-interference in the internal affairs of other states'. To us that seems unequivocal. But the boundaries are not defined in the treaty and it is quite open to the Russians to say that incursions in what we regard as non-Russian territory are merely reoccupation of their own country. We must remember that, voting on the ratification of the treaty, were representatives of the 'Lithuanian, Latvian and Esthonian Socialist Soviet Republics'. By publishing this to the world, the Kremlin gave notice that the Baltic states at least were to be regarded as Russian. Should we protest when these disputed territories are occupied, the Kremlin has a perfectly legal answer to make. Either the treaty was never properly ratified, or else it was ratified as a treaty in which 'territorial aggrandizement' did not refer to territory the claim to which has never been relinquished by Russia. If that was not our interpretation, why did we not protest at the time? A post-war protest from us would awake in Russia a sincere resentment at the interference in the domestic affairs of the U.S.S.R. by capitalistic countries.

Further the recent (February 1944) changes in the Constitution, whatever other purpose they may have, seem admirably designed to cover annexation of any neighbouring territory that Russia might consider expedient to acquire. Paragraph 18 A reads: 'Every Union Republic is entitled to enter into direct relations with foreign states, to conclude agreements with them and exchange diplomatic and consular representatives.' (At the same time it was enacted 'that the Union Republics are to organize Republican Army Formations'.) The following technique can now be practised. First there is infiltration both political and commercial. A Communist Party is organized and supplied with funds; firms trading with Russia prosper, those not doing so are squeezed. The Party, progressing as did the N.S.D.A.P. in Germany, gains control of the local government, establishes a socialist republic, and applies for admission into the Union of the Socialist Soviet Republics. When this is granted new territory is not 'annexed'; it has been taken into the empire with 'dominion status'. Constitutionally the new republic will maintain its independence and be as free as Canada or Eire to participate in or withdraw from common imperial action. Actually, of course, the Party will determine policy and the Party's programme will be drawn up in the Kremlin. We should recall that Stalin (unlike Hitler) is not the titular head of the Russian state and until 1941 held no government office, exercising his power solely as the Party boss.*

Although this constitutional change may be interpreted as a device to facilitate aggression it is not necessary to assume that, for three other objectives are not far to seek. It may be an administrative measure for a decentralization that has become advisable. Or, secondly, it may be intended to provide, psychologically, a substitute for the Third International. Communism would be the official creed in many separate nations. The third reason is one that

* On May 6, 1941 he became Chairman of the Council of People's Commissars, and since the German invasion he has been Chairman of the newly formed State Council of Defence in which ultimate military authority is vested.

suggested itself to many when the new constitution was first published: in any reincarnated League of Nations Russia could claim separate representation for each of its member republics. The last explanation should not be excluded simply because of its obviousness. It is easier to think of the ways in which Russia could use her constitution to dominate or to disrupt a League than it is to see how such intentions could be frustrated.

Thus it may seem that Stalin is approaching the post-war game with more than one card up his sleeve, but, on the other hand, he is laying his cards on the table earlier than a trickster would do. On 30 April, 1944, Moscow published the text of an agreement between the U.S.S.R. and the Czechoslovak government relative to the allocation of authority between the Soviet Army and Czech officials when the former entered the latter's territory. Clause VI reads: 'As soon as any part of the liberated territory ceases to be a zone of direct military operations, the Czechoslovak Government will take over completely the power of administration of public affairs and give the Soviet allied Commander-in-Chief through its civil and military organs every assistance and help.' The next clause contains a further abnegation of Soviet control: '...all persons belonging to the Czechoslovak military forces will be subject to Czechoslovak jurisdiction. To this jurisdiction will also be subject the civil population on Czechoslovak territory, even in the cases of crimes committed against the Soviet allied troops, except crimes committed in the zone of

direct military operations, when they will be subject
to the jurisdiction of the Soviet allied Commander-in-
Chief.' The evidence for good faith lies in the combination of their specificity with their applicability
to the immediate future. Moscow could have in-
sisted on vaguer formulations, have made the transfer
of authority conditional on order having been
sufficiently established, on the Czechoslovak authorities having sufficient police at their disposal, etc. But
the only loophole a would-be evader has left himself
is the definition of what a 'zone of direct military
operations' may be. If Russia violates this agreement the Czechoslovaks can complain to the other
Allies during a period when the latter are still in
possession of means for applying pressure on the
Kremlin. The U.S.S.R. is getting vast supplies
under lease-lend and these include—quite rightly—
a good deal that is as important for rehabilitation of
peace-time industry as for the immediate production
of munitions. So it would pay Russia to keep in the
good books of the United States and Great Britain
until lease-lend ceases. In the case of Czechoslovakia
Stalin seems to be either sincere or else as clumsy in
his hypothetical duplicity as he is credited with being
astute in other instances.

'CONVERSION' TO COMMUNISM

Reverting to possible plans for incorporation of
outside areas in the U.S.S.R., some prediction as to
treatment of the inhabitants may be made. The
people in reoccupied or newly occupied territories

will not be discriminated against because they are
Finns, Poles, Letts, etc. any more than the countless
other nationalities within the U.S.S.R. are persecuted. That is, they will be allowed their own
language and cultural peculiarities *provided* their
ideology is sound. To effect the latter the dissentients
will be simply liquidated. If there is criticism abroad
it will be viewed in Moscow as pure Capitalist prejudice for two reasons: because the measures adopted
deal with a domestic Russian problem in which the
foreigner has no right to meddle; and because heresy
has always been treated like that: conversion by
kindly arguments and persuasion is only a dishonest
Capitalist myth. The individual has no rights except
in so far as he is a loyal member of the Communist
group. Indeed 'rights' is a term belonging to
Democracy and outside the vocabulary of Communism, in which what we call 'rights' are privileges
given as a reward for service to the State and proportionate to the service.

In territories which Russian armies occupy there
may be granted spurious autonomy followed by a
manipulated plebiscite, the result of which would be
a majority in favour of Communism and union with
the U.S.S.R. This would not be in order to satisfy
conscience and to demonstrate virtue to the outer
world as would be the case with Germans, but in order
to satisfy the rank and file of Russians who will thus
be made to believe that the Poles and the Balts wanted
to join the Russian 'Kingdom of Heaven'. If this
led to conflict with foreign powers, a resultant war

would be one fought to defend these new parts of
Russia, and would thus be a war of defence and not
of aggression. It might be wrong to assume that this
attitude would not be shared by the Kremlin as well.
The party high-ups probably have a cynical view of
elections in the democratic states. In their hostility
they will over-emphasize graft and the government
control of the ballot and believe that all elections are
controlled if not by the government at least by power
groups. This will be the more likely because they
will tend to think that the average democrat is as
politically untutored as is the Russian; so the
plebiscite will be to the Kremlin as real an expression
of the country's desire for Communism as it is
feasible to obtain. The Kremlin knows that Russia
is richer than the border states not merely absolutely
but relatively: that is, the potential wealth per in-
habitant is larger. It is therefore to the advantage of
small states to join with Russia. If their governments
do not evince a desire for such union it will be
because they are corrupted by plutocratic cliques or
plutocratic foreign governments. But there is no
reason to suppose that the Kremlin attitude towards
citizens thus absorbed would be different from that
towards their own minorities—i.e. liquidation of
those who don't know what is good for them, but an
equal share in the wealth of the U.S.S.R. for those
who conform.

To us, who have been brought up democratically,
that is to have individual opinions about political
matters, and have been guided by the moral traditions

of Western Catholicism and the Protestantism that split off from it, the 'rescue' of Communists in bordering countries, who have adopted that political faith under pressure or on grounds of pure expedience, seems a most barefaced and flimsy excuse reflecting a cynicism in the 'rescuer' as well as being an insult to the intelligence of those to whom the excuse is offered. But these are judgments made by people who are ignorant of Russian history. Politics and Orthodox proselytizing were always intertwined, and 'conversion' was a formal act to an extent that is to us incredible. A man who was frightened or bribed into accepting baptism became or remained, no matter what his convictions were, a member of the Orthodox Church. It is hard for us to understand how a prelate of undoubted piety could cooperate in or connive at such conversions, and apparently regard them as valid. Possibly this is a state of mind that is correlated with the preponderance of sacramentalism in Orthodox religion. Divorced from morals, sacramentalism tends to become pure magic. The operation of an incantation or any other magical rite does not depend on the belief of the magician or of the victim. At the magical level a sacrament can be effective regardless of belief with the same certainty as we expect poisonous mushrooms to injure a man who believes them to be edible. To the Russian, therefore, there may be no moral problem involved in regarding an avowed Communist as a genuine one —for political ends.

THE EXAMPLE OF THE UKRAINE

The actual history of the absorption of the Ukraine supplies us with a model for the understanding of Soviet methods and, at the same time, demonstrates how the Germans' ideology prevents their being equally successful. The Ukraine bulks large in the belt of territory running from the Baltic to the Black Sea that through the centuries has had no settled ownership, no long period during which the people could settle down for generations on end, believing themselves to be the subjects of any one dynasty or a part of any one empire. Their last rulers were the Tsars, but, during the nineteenth and the twentieth centuries up to 1914, a nationalist movement had been nurtured; to what extent it was spontaneous and corresponded to a real cultural entity and to what extent the 'nation' was a creation of separatist intellectuals, objective historians are not prepared to state. But at any rate a local patriotism did exist when the U.S.S.R. came into being. This Ukrainian nationalization was allowed a relatively free hand until 1928. Then it was denounced as right-wing nationalism and severe reprisals were carried out. Under the formula 'Nationalistic in form—Socialist in content' nationalism was persecuted. Even more important was the '...drive to enforce wholesale collectivization of agriculture where individualistic peasant farming was strongly rooted...which led to violent resistance, mass deportations and the famine of 1932–3'. During the Party purges and in connection with the great Moscow trials of 1936–8, 'a prominent place was given to German designs on the Ukraine, in line with refurbishing of schemes for eastward expansion by Hitler, Rosenberg and the "geo-politicians"' (Sumner). Moscow won out over collectivization, and at the same time the exploitation of water power and minerals with vastly increased industrialization meant the influx of a large number of industrial workers into the Ukraine, thus changing the complexion of the population. On the other hand the maintenance of Ukrainian cultural institutions and the Ukrainian language was encouraged and there was no discrimination against Ukrainian Communists *qua* Ukrainians. Timoshenko for example is a Ukrainian and so was Vatutin.

Then came the Germans and completed the Soviet-izing of the country. Whether the purges had elimin-ated all those who were actually flirting with Germany or not, there must still have been many, hitherto inarticulate, who smarted under Moscow's tyranny. Had the Nazis played their hand with Russian skill they might have exploited these malcontents. They are not unacquainted with the technique of fomenting local disaffection, they can liquidate opponents and give authority to Quislings, but they cannot win over even a divided people (as in France for example) be-cause the Herrenvolk are incapable of treating a people defeated in battle as equals. This attitude of equality is nothing difficult for the Russian Com-munist to assume because it is genuine. He may use all kinds of methods, which we should deplore, to effect conversion, but it is only conversion he seeks —not subjugation. The war has settled Ukrainian loyalty. Its sons have won glory, its sufferings have been patently sufferings for all the U.S.S.R.; Soviet victory and Ukrainian victory are one, and its would-be rescuers have been demonstrated to be brutal slave hunters.

PSYCHOLOGICAL OBJECTIVITY AND DIPLOMACY

Of what use are psychological speculations of this type? If psychology were like one of the physical sciences its data could be expressed in numerical form, its generalizations could be translated into equations and the solving of these equations would give answers of unequivocal accuracy. In other words, corresponding to exact knowledge there could be exact prediction. But psychological conclusions are—and probably always will be—guesses, and among a number of guesses prejudice will operate to select some and exclude others. Further it is safe to predict that the same prejudice will always tend to a dogmatism in defence of the selection made that is proportionate to the actual scientific uncertainty. It might therefore be argued that psychological treatment of the problems of international relationships may be tolerated as an academic pastime but excluded from diplomacy. Unfortunately this would only make matters worse. In all human contacts, whether between individuals or between different social groups, there is always some estimate made, consciously or unwittingly, of other people's character. Inveterately we tend to project on others our own scale of values. Rated on this scale the other fellow is sensible or scatter-brained, realistic or a day-dreamer, of good taste or bad, righteous or immoral. Moreover we assume that his conduct is actuated by motives like our own. If we did such and such it would be with this or that end in view. If the other fellow alleges that his action was determined by a motive that would not operate with us, then he is charged with insincerity. For instance the Russians may well have doubted our loyalty to the Alliance when we jeopardized victory in the Battle of the Atlantic by being sensitive to Eire's rights as a neutral. According to the Russian scale of moral values such 'sentimentality' would always have to give way to considerations of national security. Again, each of us, taking over his group standard in his method of achieving a given end, draws a line between honesty and dishonesty at a different point in the scale from that chosen by some one moving in a different circle.

For instance, is the phrase *caveat emptor* to be interpreted as silence about some defect in what is to be sold, as justifying a distraction of the purchaser's attention from it, a deliberate hiding of it, or a flat lying about it? The traditions of the trade in question determine where the line is drawn. A Bond Street jeweller who employs the ruses of a horse-coper is a cheat, but that does not mean that a horse dealer who expects a purchaser to know the tricks of the trade is a dishonest man—as honesty goes. To the ordinary intelligent man who affects knowledge of human nature—and who does not?—these are truisms and they guide moral judgment in dealing with different business circles. But, alas, such principles are not allowed to operate when contact is made with unfamiliar groups. The Bond Street shopper who meets a horse dealer for the first time may come to regard him as a swindler. This illustrates the difference between the 'good judge of human nature' and the psychologist. The latter, once he establishes a general principle, gives it a general application. He says, for instance, that every social group tends to build up its own peculiar code and scale of moral values and, secondly, the larger and more isolated is any group the more does it tend to universalize these standards, to regard them as characteristic of the ethics of all human beings, or even as constituting ultimate right and wrong. This tendency to project on others our own moral judgments is, perhaps, the most important single cause of international misunderstandings. We feel that the foreigner who does something of which we do not approve must know he is doing wrong and therefore is a criminal—or else, if he threatens to do such things, he must be bluffing—because of course he is a decent chap and would not really do any such thing. That was our attitude towards the Germans prior to both the last and the present wars. Similarly, to the Germans the British are hypocrites because they profess to feel responsibility for the welfare of savages, to be interested in the elevation of subject races or the spread of self-government. As imperialism is for the German sheer acquisitiveness, he assumes that other peoples cannot be sincere missionaries as well as traders.

Post-war international problems are not going to be solved if we haver between interpreting the words and actions of foreigners as having the meaning they would have for us, or by half of us regarding some country as Utopia come true, while the other half looks on it as purgatory. A wiser approach would seem to be to judge every foreign action or utterance against the background of the traditions and trend of evolution in the government responsible for it. The word or deed that fits the ethos of the country is to be judged as genuine. The one that is incongruous with this setting is bluff and is insincere. Why cannot we believe what the foreigner says when it is just what is to be expected from his nature as revealed in his history? The answer is that we do believe it when it is comforting to hear but we stop our ears when the words are disquieting. Germany gave us ample warning before both 1914 and 1939, but those who listened, those who paid the Hun the compliment of believing him to be sincere, were decried as warmongers. One of Freud's aphorisms was that no man can lie consistently except to himself. This is probably a generalization equally true of nations. The objective foreign observer realizes that in this country only the minority is vociferous, or, very often, even vocal. So when a handful of Oxford undergraduates vote they will not fight for king and country, he is not impressed. But the subjective foreign observer, who is in the overpowering majority, evaluating this journalistic titbit according to the meaning it would have in his country where political expression is governmentally controlled, concludes that the rising generation will not fight. When it does fight, Albion has been perfidious again and once more English hypocrisy has worked its ruse successfully.

INCOMPATIBILITY OF AIMS DOES NOT NECESSITATE HOSTILITY

When German resistance ceases there will be no country whose point of view it will be more necessary to understand than that of Russia. We are fighting for a democracy, which means a freedom for individuals and for minorities, and would take it amiss if, as a result of victory in the war, peoples allied to us lost such freedoms. The Russians on the other hand are fighting in the interests of a *system*. They in their turn would take it ill if, after all their sacrifices, their system were not allowed to operate at least in all the territory where it has once been in existence. This disparity cannot be smoothed out by any Russian polite use of the word 'democracy' or by our oratory which would make the joint campaign against an obviously predatory tyranny a proof of identity in political aims. The only possible solution is compromise, a compromise that can be effected only if there is plain speaking and mutual admission of the

incompatibility of aims. We should meet at the
council table as those holding rival ideologies but
wishing to establish a *modus vivendi* and not as pre-
tended friends. The latter would almost certainly widen
the breach with unofficial talk of 'insincerity' on both
sides and prepare the way for war in the future. The
reason is that a 'friend' is inevitably viewed as a
well-wisher who wants to collaborate in the further-
ing of one's interest—and this interpretation will hold
for public opinion on both sides. So a compromise
under the guise of 'friendship' will mean an alleged
betrayal by each party of the interests of the other.
Thus a smouldering resentment will result. On the
other hand if irreconcilability of views is admitted on
both sides the accusation of treachery will not be
plausible.

Between the democracies and an aggressive
Comintern that strove to promote world-wide revolution conflict would be inevitable sooner or later.
But if Russia does go isolationist, there would be no
reason for an inevitable war. On the other hand past
events and policies have left their marks on both
sides. There have been reasons for suspicion, and
mutual hostility has become traditional in large
sections of the peoples involved. We cannot reach
the bulk of the Russian people with any effective
propaganda to convert them to our notions of the
value of individual liberty; but if we are not careful,
we may goad the Kremlin into an anti-democratic
propaganda for Russian consumption. In other
words, if we assume in our publicity and in our

diplomacy that the Third International is only shamming death we may actually revive it. Our traditional distrust is based on a very old prejudice, old enough to have been incorporated in the saying, 'Scratch a Russian and you will find a Tartar'. Then there is a connection that has been built up in people's minds between revolutionary programmes and Russia. Financiers, employers and organized labour, all of whom are liable to suffer directly and immediately from any violent change in our political and economic life, have during this generation been told by the U.S.S.R. that it was going to attack these vested interests wherever they were to be found. They have followed Moscow in making the terms Russian and Communism synonymous, and the habit of thinking they are the same will die slowly. Another influence operating to maintain incredulity as to a change in Soviet policy is the extreme Left in our midst, the people who call themselves Communists, who in the past were in contact with Russia and, in the future, will pretend they stand for what the great and powerful U.S.S.R. stands for. All these influences will have to be combated before belief will be generally accorded to the sincerity of Russia's avowed change in policy.

Chapter V

THE FUTURE OF COMMUNIST RUSSIA: INTERNAL EVOLUTION

IS RUSSIAN OPPORTUNITY MATCHED WITH STABILITY?

After uneasy contact with Western Europe for many centuries, Russia can now see a real chance of self-government untroubled by fear or envy of her Western neighbours. The two factors which make this independence possible are the end of the monarchy and industrialization. Constant intermarriage with European royal houses kept the Tsars embroiled in dynastic intrigues, even if they wished to be just Russians. Interlocking with this influence was the industrial backwardness of the country that needed foreign machines and foreign engineers—not to mention foreign capital—for the exploitation of its natural resources. That stage is now passed; Russia has beaten Germany in a war of material as well as in a war of brawn. She has every reason to feel superior to Europe and can afford to neglect it. And the stage is set for a rapid increase of wealth that may easily be more spectacular than that of the United States during the past century. The need for internal development is mandatory, enthusiasm for it is unbounded, and the opportunities for its almost limitless success are without a precedent. So we are safe in assuming that reconstruction and the creation of new wealth will proceed apace as soon as fighting ceases.

But Communist Russia is still finding herself. That is, she is still in a stage of rapid evolution. The factors listed as making a unique constellation of political and economic influences do not all tend towards stability. Moreover there are others that will inevitably appear. Although surmises as to what may happen in this vast experiment must be highly speculative they are worth making because, as onlookers, we may be dazzled by a brilliance that is temporary and be tempted into imitation of a system that might well be, of its very nature, impermanent, or, if permanent, dependent on sacrifices that we should never make if we knew what we were doing.

Stability in any country or any nation rests on two factors, basic continuity and consistency of tradition and of outlook on the part of the people, and consistency of policy pursued by the government. In democracies the former is the more important and tends to control the government whose task it is to give specific expression to what the people want. In bureaucracies, however, policy is initiated rather by the central authority, which can vary its actions within wide limits, these being set by the amenability of the populace to propaganda on the one hand and to force on the other. Since democracy rests ultimately on the habits of the citizenry holding political opinions and considering themselves as electors responsible for the government, it can never be established merely by setting up a machine for representative government but can only be a gradual process extending through generations. So, no matter what formal constitution there may be in Russia, we may be sure that, in the immediate future, its policies will be determined by whatever group or dictator within the Party is in control, appointing officials, issuing edicts and fortifying these with propaganda. Looking forward, therefore, we must distinguish between the Russia of the immediate future, a country populated by millions who have never been trained to exercise individual intellectual and moral choice, and the remoter future when the changed conditions brought about by a national socialism may have borne fruit. Even if the people remain wax in the hands of the Kremlin rulers, it would be a different wax when the average standard of comfort had been raised and illiteracy had become the exception rather than the rule.

THE DISCREPANCY BETWEEN THEORY AND PRACTICE

Assuming that Stalin remains at the helm and that the U.S.S.R. is not involved in continued fighting, the first post-war years will probably be marked by a united effort to replace destroyed assets and to proceed with the interrupted programme of economic development, education and the improvement of the standard of living. These preoccupations should preclude disunity, but the seeds of disintegration are undoubtedly present ready to germinate when and if conditions are favourable. The potentialities for discord lie in two different fields. The first is the absence of a politico-economic theory corresponding to the trend of actual evolution. Marxism and Nationalism are essentially incompatible, and, until the former is specifically jettisoned and a newer, more realistic theory is formulated, intellectuals will be shocked by the 'heresy' of what goes on or personally ambitious Party leaders may invoke the names of Marx and Lenin to excuse actions that run counter to the actual, nationalist policy. In other words, there is always the possibility of the single Party being split along lines similar to 'right' and 'left' or 'conservative' and 'liberal', because those polarities are not merely political but rest on those temperamental differences which keep exhibiting themselves in the way in which men approach all their major problems. In democracies birds of a feather are encouraged to flock together, but in countries with one-party governments such congregation means treason. If the group is small it is wiped out when discovered by the secret police. If it is larger there is unsuccessful revolt or actual revolution. The second, and perhaps more likely cause of disunion, is parochialism.

'DOMINION STATUS' IN THE SOVIET
REPUBLICS

The greatest union of states yet known is that whose components owe allegiance to the British crown. Years ago it was learned that its interests were too disparate to be centrally administered, and disintegration rather than integration has been the trend of its organizational evolution during recent generations. Yet it still shows a strong working unity when challenged. When not challenged, local differentiation in political forms and economic habits proceeds apace. Since the U.S.S.R. has adopted under its latest constitution an organization of its separate 'republics' that is, on paper, not unlike that of the British empire, students of Russia would do well to scrutinize the working of the older commonwealth. The dominions (with the exceptions of South Africa and Eire) are countries peopled chiefly with immigrants from Britain who have carried to their new homes traditions that we sum up as 'democratic', these represent ideals that are taken for granted by the inhabitants and provide no motive—at least no conscious one—for decisions and specific actions in ordinary day to day living. Local needs provide the problems for politicians in the peace-time life of the dominions; there may even be a considerable trade rivalry between them or between them and the mother country. There is, so to speak, no empire when there is peace, but it springs to life again when 'democracy' is threatened—much to the discomfiture of those who can only read the lines and never between them. Now this is obviously no model for the U.S.S.R. to follow. Its programme is so largely economic that it would be suicidal to allow the separate republics independence in their conduct of agriculture, mining and manufacture unless they were allowed to lend each other money and to invest in each other's undertakings, in other words, unless all the machinery of capitalism were reintroduced. But the Bolshevists are out to prove that a common purse will work better than a lot of purses in developing the whole country. This means that the wealth of one community must be diverted from local spending for the creation of more wealth in another, still unproductive, area. If the separate republics really had the liberty of action allotted to them under the new constitution, they would be most unlikely to submit to this expropriation.

PAROCHIALISM

It is clear, of course, how the desired unanimity of action will be achieved. The Republics are not peopled by those of the same or similar tradition in government, religion or economy. They cannot be trusted to take spontaneous action in the interest of the U.S.S.R. as a whole, but that unity will be achieved through the same channels as have been conducting government since the Soviet Union came into existence. In other words, the Central Party Executive will give directions to the Party officials in the provinces in whose hands the local government rests. Will this system be permanent? Russians—even Bolshevists—are not human unless they tend to have local loyalties, unless they tend to feel at least as strongly the needs of those they meet daily as the needs of those of different colour and religion a thousand miles away. Will the Party members in the Ukraine, when its agriculture and industries have been re-established, be content to see their wheat and machines flowing away, while their schools and hospitals are still below the desired standards? If they could only use their own wealth, local conditions could be so much improved! Moscow will, of course, say no—or else abandon its programme of nation-wide development. Thus disaffection will grow. There are only two ways I can see in which this parochialism might be prevented; neither seems adequate and both are perhaps impracticable. The local commissars might all be 'foreigners', that is drawn from the other republics. Or there might be an extension of the system whereby all juniors before appointment to the more important offices are brought to Moscow for a period of duty in the Kremlin where they are indoctrinated with an enthusiasm for the U.S.S.R. calculated to submerge their local patriotism to a greater extent.

Closely associated with the danger of local disaffection is the presence locally of the machinery for revolt. It may or may not be true that a military caste has developed during the war, but at least we may be sure that the Army has gained an enormous prestige which is unlikely to be deprecated by the leaders of the permanent military establishments when peace comes. Now under the new constitution every republic is to have its own army. Unless the recruitment both as to officers and men of each of these armies is to come from outside the republic in question—a great unlikelihood—it would be difficult to prevent the development of provincial loyalties, military as well as civil. If the local Chief Commissar and Commander-in-Chief are friends....?

CAN A SUCCESSOR TO STALIN BE FOUND?

These dangers are less threatening than the perils through which Stalin has already steered the ship of State, and it is probable that, so long as he is at the helm, with his prestige, his cold wisdom and his burning courage, there will be no trouble of this kind. But he is mortal and can no longer be called even middle-aged. When he dies or retires, the difficulties mentioned above may appear because the central controlling force will have gone. A revolution throws up great men and Russians are not a stupid lot.* A successor of equal personal ability might be found to Stalin, but, even if there is no discord-breeding rivalry for his job, it is improbable that a second man can pursue his policy. That is because it has been a policy that both anticipated, effected and followed a rapid evolution. If his successor merely goes on with what Stalin was doing during his last days in office, he will stop the evolution and before long be regarded as obstructive. If, on the other hand, he endeavours to be progressive, who can quiet the opposition based on the belief that he is departing from the policy of a Stalin who by that time will have been sainted?

* It would be by no means ridiculous to claim that in proportion to its literate population, Russia has contributed more to the arts and sciences during the past two centuries than any other country.

Perhaps the surest way of guaranteeing trouble would be for Stalin to leave a political testament. This would have to be either so vague in its terms as to make it a cover for almost any policy or else it would be specific. But no man can foresee all, and the exact nature of, the problems that will in future face his state. The testament would merely become the excuse for legalistic quarrels in which the disputants would only convince themselves by their arguments of the rightness of their interpretations.

Turning from these highly problematical conditions in the post-war years it may be worth while to look further ahead and see how the forces set in motion in modern Russia may operate in future generations.

ANALOGY WITH THE UNITED STATES

Unless the strong nationalism that the war has created or fortified is unequal in its strength to the disintegrative potentialities just mentioned, we may expect the U.S.S.R. to be soon established as the richest country in the world. Untold wealth is awaiting exploitation, serious attack on the country by an outside power is an improbability, and individual ambition has a good opportunity for reaping large rewards. The magnitude of its munitions production shows how great is the surplus manufacturing capacity available for the production of both capital and consumers' goods. As the country becomes richer, ambivalent reaction towards Europe and the world generally should diminish, for there would be little reason to maintain any feeling of inferiority, unless a materialistic outlook of the masses and of the authorities makes some intellectuals jealous of a real or imagined cultural superiority abroad. However, the numbers of such malcontents will be small and their influence trivial. The general trend will be towards an isolationist feeling of superiority similar to that of the United States before the great depression fifteen years ago, that shook American cocksureness and was, perhaps, the second great landmark in its social history after the Civil War. As in the United States there will be faulty discrimination between easy exploitation of great natural resources and real business genius. It is hard for a man who has made a fortune by stumbling on a gold mine not to imagine that he is an abler man than is his neighbour who sweats to win a bare livelihood. The Russians, we may be confident, will ascribe their wealth to the virtues of their system. Communism may or may not be the best economic system, but there cannot be a clean experiment made in Russia, for its resources are vast enough to yield incalculable wealth even if they are exploited inefficiently. The parallel with America may go further. Just as reactionary plutocrats have had a large influence in shaping the economy of that country, so in Russia there may be a danger of reactionary bureaucrats becoming entrenched in authority: the commissars under whose direction machines, oil, minerals and the spate of consumers' goods have filled the markets will have a prestige disproportionate to their personal contribution to the creation of this wealth. Still another analogy between Scythia and the Hesperides will be the supply of cheap labour. In America it came from hordes of immigrants; in Russia it will come from a fecund peasantry, largely Asiatic, ready for exploitation by the entrepreneur commissar, to be sweated, but getting with any luck a higher standard of comfort than their forebears had ever dreamed of.

But with this taste of better things will there come a demand for a 'New Deal'? Will the seed of democracy germinate? A dictatorship run for the benefit of the proletariat can endure only so long as there is a proletariat, that is a great mass of workpeople that are like dumb, driven cattle. Improve their living conditions, educate them, improve their health and, above all, give them security and leisure, and, inevitably, they will begin to think for themselves; they will cease to be serfs in mentality. They are certain to become politically minded, to want more power even if the miracle is accomplished of an equal distribution of this world's goods. Against whom will they struggle?

SOCIAL STRATIFICATION

Social and political evolution comes about through the formation of groups with common grievances or common aspirations who organize, get their spokesmen, leaders and martyrs, canvass, agitate or fight for their claims which, by a curious but unchallenged perversion in meaning, they call their 'rights'. Were it not for 'divine discontent' there would be no political evolution. What will the prosperous comrade of the future find to quarrel with? Nothing, if Utopia goes according to plan, but, if it does not, there will have appeared classes and sectional interests. It is not difficult to see how the general situation will favour sectionalism and also to discern where specific cleavages may occur.

Man as a gregarious animal is forever forming groups; one may belong to many, some small and trivial demanding little loyalty, and others, like religions and national communities, asking for and being accorded the sacrifice of life itself. When a large group is challenged its members neglect the minor loyalties and serve the major cause. What interest is not abandoned when one's country goes to war? Conversely during peace the parish may get more attention and service than the nation. Functionally the country as a whole has become insignificant. Reminders of its existence appear—as is the case with all groups—when it comes into competition with other peoples. It follows that nationalism is a conscious and motivating factor in the mind of the citizens when foreign influences are felt. Thus the more a people dwells in isolation the more will they segregate themselves into cliques, as is witnessed by the 'power groups' in American politics. The U.S.S.R., fired with the ambition to show the world that Communism can work, will be united. On the other hand, successful and isolationist Russians will tend to express their gregariousness locally and devote themselves to class or regional causes.

There are, of course, officially no classes in Russia, but, since there is government and not anarchy, there are the governors and the governed. If, as has been said before, the recruitment of the Party and of its officials remains truly indiscriminate, the aristocracy is renewed each generation and has only a personal, and not a family status. But is this likely to last? If there is one generalization about human nature that has a widespread validity, it is that parents want to do the best they can for their children. They want— to use a telltale phrase—to give them 'advantages', that is to improve their chances in competition with the sons and daughters of their neighbours. Here another human characteristic should be borne in mind. As men get older and the passions of earlier life cool, they tend to seek a kind of immortality for themselves in the careers of their children. This means that the desire for the success of their offspring is strongest at the time when, if ever, they have achieved some eminence in the community and are people of influence. If, consciously or unconsciously, this influence is not used to favour their children's admission into special schools, into putting their feet on the bottom rungs of the ladder which reaches into the successful official class, then Communism will have worked a psychological miracle. It is quite possible for a man to be a good Communist and yet seek preferment for his child conscientiously. The individual—entirely apart from the probability of his inheriting a higher intellectual capacity—who is born into the family of a successful man, has environmental advantages in extra-scholastic education that are inevitable. He overhears and eventually participates in intelligent conversation; he grows up in a family where orders are given rather than received—the existence of domestic servants is a theoretic anomaly in Russia—so the assumption of responsibility, which is essential for leadership, is not frightening to him. Finally, if the child of a commissar is not watched for potential leadership when he gets to school, then teachers in Russia must be dowered with superhuman objectivity or infrahuman stupidity.

The environment of a child is not confined to his own household. He plays with neighbours and with the children of family friends. Broadly speaking, three general factors inevitably operate to determine such social circles. They are: blood relationships, similarity of interests and economic equality. The second and third must tend towards a development of class differences. Affections formed in childhood and adolescence do not lapse, although they may weaken, when the family separates in adult life. Brothers and sisters keep in touch with each other and their children are brought together. The clan life of social circles varies enormously among different cultures in its cohesiveness, but there must always be some tendency towards its production. Similarly in adult life those who work together or at like tasks have something in common to discuss, if not to cooperate in. The more the work is intellectual rather than manual, the more does it involve problems in which collaboration and exchange of opinions are natural. So this kind of contact again tends to favour the segregation from the masses of those who give orders. Finally, there is the selective factor in the standards of comfort and externals of living. Originally, the Communists thought that all comrades should live alike, but they soon found that those who planned and organized labour cannot work efficiently—or refuse to do so—if they are not free from petty routines of living, such as can be attended to by servants, have no leisure in which to think, lose time and temper if subject to delays in transport, or are vexed by the irritations and discomforts of primitive living conditions. So their standard of comfort was raised. Now, no matter how 'democratic' a man may be he cannot easily share the life of another whose society he seeks if the other's amenities cannot be shared. Inevitably, therefore, the reward for work of different degrees of national importance tends to separate off the total body of workers into different social groups or levels. So long as the community as a whole is enthusiastically working towards a common objective, such stratification does not matter; but, if the common aim is obscured, sectional interests will become the foci of loyalty. In a word, class feeling will be developed. Those who are in authority, their children and their friends, will tend to regard themselves as a superior lot whose superiority should be suitably rewarded and perpetuated.

On the other hand, the routine workers will tend to react by resenting their exclusion from government: they will want Democracy in addition to Communism.

The original notion of the revolutionary government that free love should be substituted for marriage and that children should be wards of the State was probably a slap in the face for the moral code of the capitalistic countries, but there may have been also present in this policy an intuition of the basic psychological truth that ultimately family ties cut across pure Communism. But the authorities had to give way and, once concessions were made, more and more had to be granted. As I write it has just been announced that the divorce laws have been changed so as to make divorce more difficult. 'Bourgeois morality' has sneaked in to corrupt the purity of Communism.

KULAKS AND STAKHANOVISTS

A caste system rarely, if ever, consists simply of two classes, an upper and a lower. There is, rather, a multiple stratification, which is probably inevitable with the successive delegation of authority that occurs in every organization, military or economic. One of the complaints against capitalism made by the moderate socialists (who admit the legitimacy of different rates of pay for different kinds of service) is that it favours the exploitation of labour; that is, increased production does not lead to proportionate improvement in the lot of the worker. All, or too much of the surplus goes to the entrepreneur. This may or may not be true, but it seems to be demonstrated in Soviet Russia that the fundamental trouble may be the inveterate human tendency to abuse power, because there an analogous exploitation occurs without the use of the capitalistic mechanism. It has appeared in both the agricultural and industrial fields although with different results—to date.

Prior to the revolution—and one of the causes of the unrest that led to it—the stratification of the peasant population was notorious. The Russian village contained three classes, the kulaks, the middle peasants and a poverty-stricken group of farm labourers. The kulak was a mixture of small farmer, landlord, middleman and usurer. His name indicates the esteem in which he was held, for *kulak* in Russian means 'fist'. During the first years of Bolshevik rule an attempt was made to abolish this anomaly in a 'classless society'. But agricultural production sank to famine levels—owing to a great variety of causes —and under the New Economic Policy the kulaks were encouraged to resume their old functions. Once more they enlarged their farms at the expense of their less successful neighbours, let land to middle peasants which they could not farm themselves, hired the indigent as labourers and, above all, marketed all the crops that were locally produced. The return to the old order rescued agriculture from its agony but there it stuck. The kulaks were opposed to mechanization, which alone could greatly increase production but which involved large-scale farming. So, under the Five-Year Plans Stalin liquidated them. They did not go down without a struggle: by refusing to sow and by killing off their beasts they almost succeeded in starving the country into submission—famine deaths are said to have been 4 million in 1932–3. But they were eventually, and with cold-blooded ruthlessness, utterly defeated. In their place came collective farms and State buying-agencies.

This seems to be a victory for socialism and for Communist principles. But no sooner had the kulaks been liquidated than there began a development in industry of something suspiciously like the kulak system. If we are to believe E. Strauss (*Soviet Russia*, 1941)—and he seems to have gone thoroughly into the subject—*Stakhanovism* in reality and Stakhanovism as revealed in Kremlin propaganda are by no means identical. According to the propaganda the Stakhanovist is a workman who, patriotically inspired by greater zeal, ingenuity and industry, increases his output and for this service is paid higher wages and honoured by his fellows and by the State. Actually, it is said, there is more in the system than just individual ardour, for the scheme also involves the principle of what we call 'dilution'. The skilled worker is freed from the necessity of performing any but skilled manipulations; all the unskilled work (previously part of his job) is done by a team of ordinary workmen under him. The increased production is not reflected in increased wages for the group as a whole but the reward goes to the Stakhanovist alone. This takes the form of higher wages—up to ten-fold, it is

said—but the chief benefits are secondary in the form
of special privileges. In Soviet Russia rationing
guarantees the distribution of basic necessities while
'luxuries' of all kinds are purchasable in 'free' shops
or only by those licensed to acquire them, among
whom are to be found the Stakhanovists as well as
officials. 'The contrast between the Red Director,
who received a cash premium for the financial results
of "his" enterprise, and the workers as a whole was
reproduced in every workshop.... Wages of 800,
1000, 1200 and more roubles a month are not unusual
for Stakhanovists of repute [as compared with a basic
wage of 125] and the "heroes of labour" tell in inter-
views in the Soviet Press about motor cycles and cars,
wireless sets and gramophones, private lessons in
dancing or in foreign languages, and many other good
things which they are now able to enjoy...many of
them were distinguished by the highest honours and
were accepted as members of the leading strata of the
ruling bureaucracy.... Only a little more than a year
after the beginning of the Stakhanov movement, in the
8th Soviet Congress in December 1936, no less than
371 Stakhanovists were enrolled among the 2016
delegates' (Strauss).

It has always been charged against capitalism that
it led to the exploitation of the many by the gifted or
favoured few. But the Stakhanovist system seems to
indicate that this is an unlovely characteristic of
human nature which may be used by a Communist
state, as well as by the capitalist, to serve its ends. In
the countries where economy is in the hands of

private capitalists in whole or in part, the trade union fights against this 'rugged individualism'. But in Russia trade unions have lost the right to fight for the common man, and there is no answer except revolt in some form or another. Revolt, however, can become a reality only when it has leaders, and the Stakhanovist system bribes the potential leader of the proletariat to enter the ranks of the aristocracy. So it is a good device for the maintenance of a reactionary regime. So good is it that it is not surprising to find that it was introduced (or reintroduced?) on the collective farms just before the war.

A POSSIBLE CHANGE IN ORTHODOXY

A factor which may also have its repercussion on the general Russian policy of the future is the evolution of Orthodoxy. In many aspects of its life, and conspicuously in the religious one, Russia was still in the Middle Ages at the time of the revolution. What the Reformation did for Christianity in Western Europe may be accomplished in the East by the persecution and disestablishment which Orthodoxy has suffered. This medievalism was exhibited in two quite different ways. One was the worldly interests of the established church. It owned much property and was deeply involved in politics, its hold over the people being exploited by the government on the one hand, while on the other it had some influence on the Tsar and his advisers, although the latter varied greatly from time to time. The other anachronism was the degree in which the 'magical' side of its sacramentalism was allowed to exist. Few of us seem to be totally without superstition although we are shamefaced about it and—except perhaps during the perils of war—do not let portents and charms affect our life seriously. But in Russia the coincidence of Christian faith with belief in all kinds of nature spirits, demons and fairies and the practice of witch-craft in some form or another was so common that the Russians had a technical term for it, which can best be translated as 'double-belief'. With this sur-vival of paganism in the form of tolerated super-stition it was only natural that Orthodoxy was, for a vast number of adherents, only another form of magic, the use of procedures that were effective in themselves to procure paradise in the absence of true spirituality or morality. Side by side with this crude magic there were also, of course, many truly religious people, including mystics and theologians; but so there were in the Middle Ages.

The political temptations of the church simply disappeared with the revolution. To be a priest was to be a fifth wheel in the Bolshevist economic system, a useless appendage. The priest had to live on the charity of the hard-pressed faithful. These were conditions to test faith, and the survivors must be those of robust spiritual stature. The same is true of the flock. A penniless ragged magician who sells safe-conducts to paradise or changes the weather has little prestige—when the peasants wanted magic they would go to a plausible mountebank. In a word persecution inevitably tends not only to rob a church of its worldly possession, but also to stamp out all its philandering with temporal interests. What remains is either nothing or it is true religion. The survivors have gained from their worship no magical escape from earthly woes but fortitude to bear them. This must tend to bind together the faithful in sympathy and mutual aid, a situation likely to foster the moral aspect of religion. But another factor will also tend in the same direction—although negatively. An element in the anti-God campaign was a fight against superstition which, although motivated by a belief in materialism, may have had some religious value when challenging Orthodoxy to show that it was not just magic. For various reasons, therefore, we may expect future Russian religion to be purified of its dross and exert influence of a moral kind. What effect may this have on politics?

CHRISTIANITY AND DEMOCRACY

One of the major factors in differentiating East from West is the attitude towards the cheapness or value of human life. To this Christianity has contributed no small influence. To the Christian every human being has a soul to be saved and, whether his social status is high or low, the task of evaluating the soul is left to God. In other words Christianity gives the individual a dignity that has much to do with the development of democracy. Should Orthodoxy begin to stress the moral aspect of religious duty, the obligation one has to one's fellows, this will tend to elevate the status of the individual, he will no longer be an undifferentiated unit in a mass that is treated as a totality. So crude Communist practices in the liquidation of individuals, villages, economic groups or whole tribes that refuse the Kremlin's planning may shock the moral sentiment of the future Russian as it does less oriental people.

RIVALRY WITH CHINA

All the factors discussed will have a disintegrating action, as has been explained, largely in so far as Russia breaks contact with the outside world and achieves a real isolation. The prospect of this in the West is favourable, but the same may not be true in the East. For centuries expansion has been eastward —at one time the Russians had not only crossed the Pacific and settled in Alaska, their trading settlements extended even so far as California. The Russo-Japanese war seemed to threaten a permanent restriction of Russian expansion towards the Pacific, but what is left of Japan at the end of this war is unlikely to challenge the Communist penetration. China is more of a problem.

A China that had died but no one bothered to bury has provided a modern miracle. Following the precedent of Nippon the Chinese have been turning to the West for education in technical matters. At first modernization brought only destruction of old values and disunity. But then the Japanese invasion led to a nationalization of the empire that few had thought possible. United and mechanized, to what heights may not the Chinese rise with millenniums of wisdom behind them? Here is something for the Russians to view with apprehension if not alarm. The U.S.S.R. has been wounded sorely by Germany and will doubtless requite that injury so far as is possible. At any rate the present struggle has advanced Russian prestige, not reduced it. But twice the Communists have had their face slapped. Once was by Poland who threw back the Red Army in 1920. The second insult was from the present Generalissimo of China who threw out the Communists. It would be strange if the Kremlin forgot that. A *casus belli* is not far to seek. Between what is indubitably China in the east and Russia in the west is a vast territory of undetermined boundaries inhabited largely by nomads of many races. Infiltration from either direction is practically certain to lead to friction between the two resurgent empires and, quite possibly, war. It is in this direction and not towards the West, that imperialist tendencies may show themselves operating to weaken or indeed to destroy Russia's isolationism. This will be the test as to whether the U.S.S.R. wishes to be a pacific power or, like most empires, will not know where to stop her expansion. Before many years we shall see whether the Communists are prepared to tolerate a rival power in Asia or not. If China's future seems doubtful, Russia will stake, and establish by force of arms if need be, a more or less reasonable claim in the disputed border zone. On the other hand, if China seems to be going ahead as Japan did when westernized, the same quarrel may be made the pretext for carrying the war on till the budding power is crippled. It will not be difficult to find Quislings. Some Ma Chung Ying will appear from nowhere to free his compatriots from the thraldom of Capitalism. On the other hand such fears may prove to be merely conjured up by us out of memories of what Russia has been in the past and it may be that, if we could read the present with that past, we should see a power that had already sown its wild oats and was approaching a manhood which would prove to be more respectable than its rebellious youth and vastly more virtuous than its forebears.

Russia's fate is in Russian hands to an extent unprecedented in modern history; but in so far as we can affect her evolution it will certainly not be by treating her either as an angel or as a devil. We should rather, look on her as human, perhaps all too human. Russians, like ourselves, have their virtues and their vices, but differ from us in what they consider to be morally admirable, indifferent or repugnant. Peaceful relations depend on tolerance, and tolerance must rest on knowledge of what is to be tolerated—on both sides.

INDEX

CAMBRIDGE: PRINTED BY W. LEWIS, M.A., AT THE UNIVERSITY PRESS